CUSTOMER TESTIMONIALS

Dear David,

Your artisanal pencil you sent me for free stabbed me in the neck. I am not happy with it. It is too sharp, too perfectly hand-shaped for violence, too much care and time was put into it to craft the prettiest, most arrogant pencil I've ever met.

I felt it sneering at me, laughing at my uneducated, unsophisticated idiocy and I had to stab myself in the ... I mean, and then it stabbed me in the neck.

Unsatisfied customer,
SPIKE JONZE (filmmaker)

The hand-sharpened pencils sent to me by artisanal pencil sharpener David Rees are without a doubt the most efficient writing instruments in my collection. I use them both for business and for pleasure, as their sleek and elegant design coupled with their amazing sharpness help make me an object of envy at work and about town.

—MATT TAIBBI, investigative journalist

Of all the artisanal crafts, hat blocking, cobbling, and trolloping, I think I was most disheartened to see pencil sharpening relegated to the dusty bin of history. That is why I am so thrilled David Rees is picking up the reins of the forgotten art of manual point-crafting. I love my pencil!

—AMY SEDARIS, crafts expert

Looking back, I cannot believe that I spent so many years of my life mechanically sharpening my own pencils with pencil sharpeners. Truly, my life before I was presented with correctly sharpened pencils by an artisan was a dull and ill-sharpened void. Learn from my mistakes.　　—NEIL GAIMAN, writer

A good friend was thoughtful enough to send me the gift of a David Rees artisanally sharpened pencil. I was blown away when I saw it. My wife and I proudly display it in our home. I have always been a pen man, but if you've got to have a pencil in the house, this is the pencil to have.

—PAUL F. TOMPKINS, actor/comedian

BEST SHARPENED PENCIL IN MY LIFE EVER!
—MIKE WATT, musician

Thank you for the artisanally sharpened pencils David Rees. They look very phenomenal. They were so sharp. I was so flabbergasted when I saw them. They were amazing. I was so astonished.
—BESS, 3rd grader

The university gallery where I've worked as director for over 20 years oversees an ambitious program of rotating art exhibitions and a permanent collection of over 7,000 art objects and artifacts. When I saw David Rees's artisanally sharpened pencils, I knew immediately to buy one for my personal collection.
—CATHERINE TEDFORD, university art gallery director

My son knows how much I appreciate two things: fine art, and any form of writing that can be erased later if circumstances warrant. This led him to generously give me an Artisanal Pencil for Christmas. His gift, however, has burdened me with fears of miscalculation: Should I use it ceaselessly and without shame, grinding its point of perfection to dust? Or should I frame and mount my pencil as the fine work of art that it is?
—DOUGLAS K. GERMAN, actuary

As a craftsman and teacher I strive to show my students fine work; I believe it inspires them. Though I dare not use Mr.

A good friend was thoughtful enough to send me the gift of a David Rees artisanally sharpened pencil. I was blown away when I saw it. My wife and I proudly display it in our home. I have always been a pen man, but if you've got to have a pencil in the house, this is the pencil to have.

—PAUL F. TOMPKINS, actor/comedian

BEST SHARPENED PENCIL IN MY LIFE EVER!

—MIKE WATT, musician

Thank you for the artisanally sharpened pencils David Rees. They look very phenomenal. They were so sharp. I was so flabbergasted when I saw them. They were amazing. I was so astonished.

—BESS, 3rd grader

The university gallery where I've worked as director for over 20 years oversees an ambitious program of rotating art exhibitions and a permanent collection of over 7,000 art objects and artifacts. When I saw David Rees's artisanally sharpened pencils, I knew immediately to buy one for my personal collection.

—CATHERINE TEDFORD, university art gallery director

My son knows how much I appreciate two things: fine art, and any form of writing that can be erased later if circumstances warrant. This led him to generously give me an Artisanal Pencil for Christmas. His gift, however, has burdened me with fears of miscalculation: Should I use it ceaselessly and without shame, grinding its point of perfection to dust? Or should I frame and mount my pencil as the fine work of art that it is?

—DOUGLAS K. GERMAN, actuary

As a craftsman and teacher I strive to show my students fine work; I believe it inspires them. Though I dare not use Mr.

CUSTOMER TESTIMONIALS

Dear David,

Your artisanal pencil you sent me for free stabbed me in the neck. I am not happy with it. It is too sharp, too perfectly hand-shaped for violence, too much care and time was put into it to craft the prettiest, most arrogant pencil I've ever met.

I felt it sneering at me, laughing at my uneducated, unsophisticated idiocy and I had to stab myself in the . . . I mean, and then it stabbed me in the neck.

Unsatisfied customer,
SPIKE JONZE (filmmaker)

The hand-sharpened pencils sent to me by artisanal pencil sharpener David Rees are without a doubt the most efficient writing instruments in my collection. I use them both for business and for pleasure, as their sleek and elegant design coupled with their amazing sharpness help make me an object of envy at work and about town.

—MATT TAIBBI, investigative journalist

Of all the artisanal crafts, hat blocking, cobbling, and trolloping, I think I was most disheartened to see pencil sharpening relegated to the dusty bin of history. That is why I am so thrilled David Rees is picking up the reins of the forgotten art of manual point-crafting. I love my pencil!

—AMY SEDARIS, crafts expert

Looking back, I cannot believe that I spent so many years of my life mechanically sharpening my own pencils with pencil sharpeners. Truly, my life before I was presented with correctly sharpened pencils by an artisan was a dull and ill-sharpened void. Learn from my mistakes.   —NEIL GAIMAN, writer

Rees's superbly sharpened #2 pencil, I proudly use it as a talking point for showcasing fine work and supporting the exemplary craftsmen who endeavor to do it. Every time I see the careful attention paid to such a simple tool, I'm reminded to spend the extra effort to do my best work.

—TREVOR WALSH, model-making and
prototyping professor/hobby wood craftsman

David Rees carved away the wood that hides the graphite the way I need to carve away the fat the hides my ability to wear a bathing suit. Thank you for showing me the path, Rees.

—PATTON OSWALT, actor/comedian

My artisanally sharpened pencil is prominently displayed in my office. Students often ask why it's there. The conversation often takes off in unexpected, interdisciplinary, and profitable new directions. Sociological: What place should handicraft occupy in the post-industrial age? Rabbinic: What is the meaning of work, and may one sharpen on the Sabbath? Aesthetic: How should we account for the surprising beauty of a properly sharpened #2 yellow pencil? Epistemological: Can the non-expert independently verify the sharpness rating (8/10, in my case) assigned by the artisan? Metaphysical: Is the pencil a "tool" if it remains on display; is it, say, what Heidegger might have called *zuhanden* (ready-to-hand)? In short, the pencil has provided many teachable moments. I highly recommend David Rees's service to other educators.

—RON MOURAD, professor of religious studies

Your pencils are awesome! If I were a pencil I would pay a lot for you to sharpen me. They were very helpful for the (state standardized) test. Thank you! Your pencils are sharp!

—ALLEGRA, 4th grader

My home burned down and most of my belongings were destroyed. As we sifted through the rubble, to my delight, I found my artisanally sharpened pencil, still in its case, completely unscathed. Many professionals arrived quickly, ready to help, but none appeared to bring a writing utensil. When asked if I had a writing utensil, I would secretly rub the artisanally sharpened pencil hiding in my pocket. Thank you David.

—LESLEY A. HAUSE, advertising manager

I gave an artisanally sharpened pencil to my wife as a wedding present. The gesture touched her very deeply. Thank you, David Rees, for demonstrating the loving care and attention to detail that lends a touchstone to the abundance of hope and meaning in our simple lives.

—JEFFREY CREALOCK-MARSH, farm representative

Could I sharpen my own pencils? Sure, I could! I could also perform my own dentistry, cobble my own shoes and smith my own tin—but why not leave such matters to real artisans, instead? I trust my bespoke pencils only to David Rees.

—ELIZABETH GILBERT, writer

In contracting, they say a good carpenter is only as good as his tools and, paradoxically, that a good carpenter never blames his tools. The elemental tool in any toolbox is the pencil; it's the one most often stolen on a job site. All projects begin with a pencil line. The accuracy of that line will incrementally lead to either the success or failure of a given project. I would never dream of bringing my artisanally sharpened pencil to a construction site—but it is a daily reminder that my tools are an extension of my professional self; they must be sharpened and maintained, as every mark reverberates into the future.

—GEORGE MANSFIELD, contractor

As a Canadian journalist, I can confirm that your pencil is useful in the real world of the Great White North. During a Manitoba winter, it's impossible to take notes in pen, because the ink will freeze. Only a pencil gets the job done. When I tackle an out-of-doors interview, I know that the notes I take will be both accurate and complete. It is a journalistic axiom that the pen is mightier than the sword. Thank you, David Rees, for putting the pencil above them both.

—GRANT A. HAMILTON, journalist

You may think that sharpening a pencil is easy, but David Rees makes it look hard, and that makes all the difference.

—JOHN HODGMAN, writer

As a luthier building instruments for some of the finest classical guitarists in the world, my profession involves absolute precision to the 10th of a millimeter. This pencil, expertly sharpened by Rees, not only provides the accuracy required for my exacting tolerances, it is a companion in my artistic process. I find each use of the pencil to be an inspirational pleasure.

—STEPHAN CONNOR, luthier

It's the sharpest pencil I've ever seen! It's perfect!

—GAIL VASQUEZ, the author's postal clerk

The artisanally sharpened pencils were absolutely flabbergasting! Question: What is your favorite tropical fruit?

—NAILAH, 3rd grader

HOW TO
SHARPEN PENCILS

A practical and theoretical treatise on the
artisanal craft of pencil sharpening, for writers,
artists, contractors, flange turners, anglesmiths,
and civil servants, with illustrations showing
current practice

———

DAVID REES

With a Foreword by
JOHN HODGMAN

MELVILLE HOUSE
Brooklyn, New York

HOW TO SHARPEN PENCILS

Book design by Christopher King

First Melville House Printing: January 2012

Melville House Publishing
145 Plymouth Street
Brooklyn, New York 11201
mhpbooks.com

ISBN: 978-1-61219-040-2

Printed in the United States of America
2 3 4 5 6 7 8 9 10

Library of Congress Cataloging-in-Publication Data

Rees, David.
 How to sharpen pencils / David Rees.
   p. cm.
 ISBN 978-1-61219-040-2
 1. American wit and humor. 2. Pencils. I. Title.
 PN6165.R44 2012
 818'.602--dc23

2011053356

TABLE OF CONTENTS

(continues)

For Margaret and Philip Rees,
the sharpest people I know.

*The simple physical artifact
multiplies the power of the individual.*
—Henry Petroski, "The Pencil: A History
of Design and Circumstance"

DAVID REES'S
ARTISANAL
PENCIL
SHARPENING, INC.

MAIL NO.2 PENCILS TO: P.O.BOX 109 BEACON, NY 12508

ONLY $12.50 PER PENCIL

each pencil will get my closest attention!

FOREWORD
BY JOHN HODGMAN

GREETINGS. My name is John Hodgman.

Look. I know it makes me a cliché. But I simply *believe* in artisanal products.

Whenever possible, I only buy meat that has been raised locally, murdered humanely, and sold in packages that have cool, contemporary, internet-style fonts on them.

When I eat cheese, which is often, I like knowing that it has been made at one of the many dairy farms that are near my summer retreat in Western Massachusetts. Not only am I supporting hardworking neighbors whom I do not know and will never meet, but also, when you eat a small production cheese, it's like you can taste the very grass that the cow herself ate. And because I am a sophisticated person, thinking about the stomach contents of a cow does not make me vomit.

When I require a tea cosy in the shape of the great tentacled head of the dread god Cthulu, I turn to Etsy. I know I could save a LOT of money if I just went down to the Old Ones By Martha Stewart aisle at Target. But I'd prefer to get something hand-knitted by a quirky, tattooed lady hipsterprenuer from Bushwick.[1]

And it is true that I also live in Brooklyn, a true Artisanal City which, neighborhood by neighborhood, brick

---

[1] Also the cyclopean architecture and impossible geometry of the Old Ones aisle at Target drives me INSANE.

by brick, is being lovingly re-crafted by a thousand skilled gentrifiers, all working together to turn every bodega into a hand-milled denim boutique, every coffee shop into an antique cocktail apothecary, and every diner into a small-batch mayonnaise salon.

And even though I am no longer a professional writer[2] I still enjoy a well-made pencil, lovingly hand-sharpened by a skilled craftsperson in Beacon, NY — not some Chinese teenager in a faraway factory.

Now, you may call paying a premium for such products the fancy of a deranged millionaire, and to some degree you'd be ABSOLUTELY CORRECT.

But there is more to artisanal products than simple status flaunting and self-congratulation, as great as those things are.

These products connect us to a more intimate, more human economy. They return us to a time not long past when ALL food, furniture, clothing, and office supplies were made, fashioned, and sharpened by people we *knew*, no matter how terrible they were at it.

When I buy these products, I am not just consuming, I am supporting a philosophy and a community. I may not know each craftsperson personally, but I can have faith that that person is probably a well-educated, photogenic white person who probably doesn't care all that much about sports. FOR US, BY US, as they say.

That is why I have always been a fan, admirer, and

---

[2] As a famous minor television personality, I outsource all my writing duties to a team of children in Indonesia.

client of the renowned artisanal pencil sharpener, David Rees. If you have encountered his work, you know that there is just something special about a bespoke-point pencil. A Rees pencil offers something more, what Walter Benjamin called the aura of the authentic: the knowledge that Rees himself labored personally over your pencil, the pleasure in knowing that with every word you write and scan-tron sheet you fill out with your custom sharpened pencil, you are destroying his hard work, bit by bit.

But while the artisanal movement enjoyed something of a hey day in the heady, debt-fueled economy of the 2000s, we are now in a recession. You may wonder how a small proprietor like Rees can survive in an economy where people may not be able to spend $12.50 on a sharpened pencil, and maybe are just burning all their pencils for warmth, or to heat up a small cup of eraser soup.

That is when Rees reveals his true nature. For unlike SOME pencil sharpeners, he is not a rank capitalist. Rather, David is so committed to the craft that he would compromise his own sharpening livelihood in order to teach you how to sharpen your own pencils. Yes: he is literally giving his trade secrets away, by selling them in a book.

In the forthcoming pages you will learn everything Rees has learned about pencil sharpening. Not only will you learn the tools and techniques of pencil sharpening, but also its metaphysics.

For, like the Buddhists and some other people, Rees knows that it is the most menial of tasks that are often most profound.

Now, a quick word to those who think this is a joke.

There are those who say that Rees, formerly known for his political clip art cartoons, was just joking around when he became an artisanal pencil sharpener. But everyone who knows Rees and his sense of humor also knows that he is a person who takes EVERYTHING VERY SERIOUSLY.

Even when he was a cartoonist, he somehow found a way to make a comic strip about the war on terror not only hilarious, but also, rage provoking and cathartic. In a culture dominated by Internet snark and fatalism, David has always been unapologetically sincere. In refusing to be jokey and cynical about war, he showed that he is unafraid to demand simple human decency and peace on earth. You think this is the kind of guy who is going to settle for a dull pencil?

So yes. YOU WILL LEARN THE PROPER WAY TO SHARPEN A PENCIL in this book. No joke.

But more, it will be your introduction to a unique mind, a true craftsperson, and in my mind, a natural treasure.

But even if you do not follow his precise instructions, apron-tying precepts, and eye-wear recommendations, David hopes, and I do, that you will at least see this: while a pencil is about accepting that there is error in life, a freshly sharpened pencil is about starting over, and never ceasing to hope for — and work for — the perfect point. While that perfection may never be attained, it is cowardly not to try.

You might as well use a felt-tip marker.

That is all.

CHAPTER 1:
SUPPLIES

THE PENCIL SHARPENER'S TOOL KIT

Just as a chef always travels with his or her favorite knives, a professional pencil sharpener — or serious enthusiast — should always have his or her tool kit ready at hand.

Fortunately, the items needed for sharpening a pencil are not expensive: I bought everything I needed for less than $1,000. Most of my pencil-sharpening kit fits inside a handsome valise I found on the side of the road.

Here are the necessary tools for pencil-pointing. Do not attempt the craft without these items.

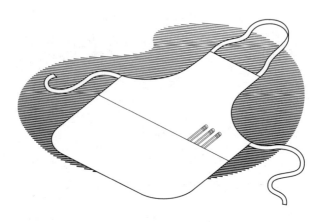

PENCILS

Pencils are crucial to our enterprise. Although it's preferable for clients to provide their own pencils, you should always have some on hand for those who don't.

Any pencil-sharpening kit should include a batch of unused #2 pencils.

SMOCK

After pencils, the most important element of my sharpening kit is my smock. A man wearing a smock, after all, is a man who means business.

Cleaning, ironing, and donning one's smock before sharpening pencils is a bit of pageantry that prepares the mind for the task at hand. It's especially helpful for live events in which multiple pencils are sharpened in sequence: Pencil sharpening is a dirty business.

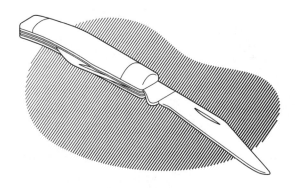

POCKETKNIFE

A pocketknife is the most straightforward way to sharpen a pencil, if not the easiest to master.

I use my late grandfather's pocketknife for clients who request a hand-hewn pencil. My grandfather was born in 1906 and didn't use calculators (my mother told me he didn't trust them). Needless to say, his calculations were worked out in pencil.

I have a vivid memory of my grandfather giving me a hand-made wooden 9-volt battery holder for Christmas. (I used to be obsessed with 9-volt batteries.) This item is not required for pencil sharpening.

TWEEZERS

I use tweezers for one of the unheralded pleasures of sharpening a pencil: collecting shavings in the job's aftermath.

(Don't trust a pencil sharpener who doesn't offer to return your shavings. The shavings are part of your pencil, after all, which means they are your property.)

During face-to-face sharpening jobs, the tweezers add a vaguely sterile, medical element to the proceedings that clients find reassuring. It's not hard to come by a good pair of tweezers; I use the ones my wife left behind when she moved out.

BAGS FOR SHAVINGS

A 3" × 4" bag will hold an entire pencil's shavings regardless of sharpening technique.

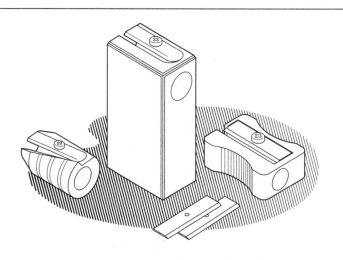

SINGLE-BLADE POCKET SHARPENERS / REPLACEMENT BLADES

Every sharpening kit should include single-blade pocket sharpeners as well as replacement blades. The pocket sharpeners I keep close at hand are:

• Alvin Brass Bullet: a hefty, well-machined device, this is my favorite pocket sharpener.

• Bethge sharpener: this German sharpener has perhaps the best hand-feel of any object I've ever used.

• United States Census-issued plastic sharpener: I rarely use this sharpener on jobs; I keep it in my kit as a reminder of my business's humble origins. (It was while working for the United States Census that I re-discovered my love of sharpening pencils.)

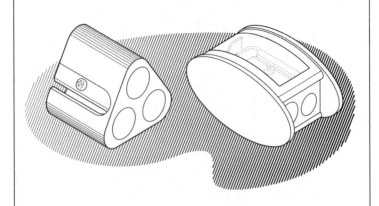

MULTIPLE-HOLE, MULTIPLE-STAGE
POCKET SHARPENERS

These devices use the same engineering as single-blade pocket sharpeners, in that the pencil is sharpened by rotating its point against a tiny blade. These sharpeners, however, feature a second blade for sharpening the graphite point after the first blade has honed the wood.

Here are the multiple-hole, multiple-stage sharpeners I use most:

• Alvin triple-hole magnesium sharpener: This model includes a third "standard" blade for people who can't be bothered to use two separate blades.

• Palomino-KUM Long Point Pencil Sharpener: A recent addition to my travel kit, this two-step sharpener produces a lovely, long point.

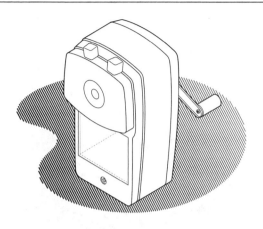

SINGLE-BURR HAND-CRANK SHARPENER

For many Americans, the first pencil sharpener they used regularly was a hand-crank model attached to a classroom wall.

As it's difficult to carry around a wall, I use table-ready hand-crank sharpeners.[1]

Everyone needs single-burr hand-crank sharpeners in his or her kit.

• The Dahle 166: Often used for oversized colored pencils, it puts a fine point on a standard #2 pencil. This is the pencil sharpener I use for my red documentation pencils (see page 25).

• The CARL Angel-5 Royal (pictured): Leaves pencils with an especially long point—longer than the Dahle. A friend brought me this model from Tokyo.

---

[1] Although I don't use wall-mounted sharpeners in my practice, their use will be discussed in Chapter 15.

DOUBLE-BURR HAND-CRANK SHARPENER

El Casco M430-CN: This is the finest hand-crank pencil sharpener in the world.

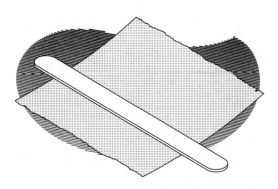

SANDPAPER / EMERY BOARD

Sandpaper is a controversial topic in the pencil-sharpening world — some pencil users keep a sheet of sandpaper close to their work area, refreshing their pencil points with a few swipes across the sheet. Sandpaper, however, can weaken a pencil point even as it sharpens it, by introducing irregular divots into the graphite. I often refine a point on plain paper, rather than sandpaper. If I do use sandpaper, I use 220-grit or 320-grit.

There is one use for sandpaper that is uncontroversial: exposing the graphite core of a pencil whose end is compromised by sloppy finishing and paint overruns. It's for this reason, even more than point-finishing, that you will always find sheets of sandpaper in my kit.

Collar imperfections can be eliminated with the delicate application of an emery board. Care must be taken, however, lest the conical surface of the pencil point is flattened or otherwise degraded by a heavy hand.

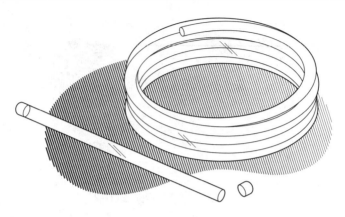

VINYL TUBING

⅜" × ¼" vinyl tubing is perfectly sized for fitting around sharpened pencil tips. Even if the client doesn't require a display tube, a protective sheath is a must. (Unless, of course, the client intends to start using the pencil immediately.)

SHATTER-PROOF PLASTIC
TUBES / CAPS FOR TUBES

8-inch plastic tubes are long enough for most #2 pencils. These tubes keep pencils safe in transit, and also double as display tubes for those clients who choose not to use their artisanally sharpened pencils. Over the course of shipping hundreds of pencils to customers, I've yet to receive a complaint of a broken pencil. The credit is due entirely to these tubes.

Please use plastic tubes to protect your pencils!

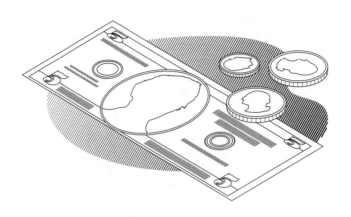

FIVE DOLLARS AND CHANGE

I always keep an extra $5.25 – $5.80 squirreled away in my pencil sharpening kit. It's the ideal amount of money: Enough to buy a sandwich if I feel light-headed, but not so much that I'll be tempted to go to the theatre instead of attending to the task at hand.

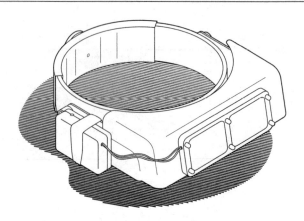

HEADBAND MAGNIFIER (WITH LED LIGHTS)

Pencil sharpening requires long stretches of close work, which can strain the eyes. A good desk-mounted or headband magnifier allows for hours of focus with minimal eye strain. I use a magnifier with 2x optical power.

What looks like a fine point under normal conditions may, under the illumination of a magnifying lens, reveal itself as less than ideal, playing host to imperfections that should be resolved before returning the pencil to its owner.

On the other hand, donning magnifying spectacles and confirming that a point really is as fine as you expect is enough to make the most hardened pencil sharpener fall into an ecstasy.

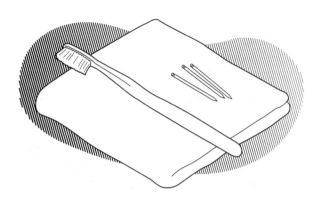

TOOTHBRUSH / TOOTHPICKS / HANDKERCHIEF

I use a toothbrush to remove graphite and wood residue from the burrs of my hand-crank sharpeners. It's always tempting to dislodge residue by banging the sharpener against a hard surface; I don't recommend this, as you run the risk of damaging the planetary gears or otherwise compromising the sharpener's mechanism. Once you use a toothbrush to clean a pencil sharpener, you should no longer use it to clean your teeth.

Wooden toothpicks are my preferred means of dislodging shavings from single-blade pocket sharpeners. Using a thumbtack, pin, or sewing needle is to be discouraged, as the metal could damage the sharpener's blade.

I use a white cotton handkerchief for removing graphite residue from a finished pencil point (sometimes called "ragging it off"), as well as the light cleaning of a pencil sharpener's exterior.

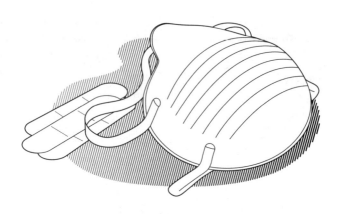

DUST MASK / BANDAGES

A dust mask is recommended for those pencil sharpeners with sensitive noses, those with a propensity for coughing, and those with life-threatening allergies to pencils.

It also makes it harder for clients to read your facial expression during a face-to-face sharpening, which can be useful.

I've injured myself only once in the course of my pencil-sharpening business: I used a dull pair of scissors to cut vinyl tubing and wound up slicing into the interdigital fold between my index and middle fingers. It was an inauspicious start to my enterprise, and a painful reminder of the importance of paying close attention to every step of the sharpening process.

Nobody wants another man's blood on his pencil.

LABELS / CERTIFICATES / RED PENCIL

Every pencil I sharpen is returned with extensive documentation. My information labels include Job Number, Date, Sharpness Rating, and other information that may be of interest to the client. I use a red pencil for recording the information and entering the job number in my log.

To be safe, I generate two labels per job order: one for the pencil tube and one for the shavings bag. If I'm fulfilling multiple orders in one sitting, recording the job numbers on both pencil and shavings eliminates the risk that a client will receive shavings that don't correspond to their pencil. (This is especially useful at parties or other chaotic environments in which the consumption of alcohol has occurred.)

Finally, each pencil is returned with a Certificate of Sharpness, stating that it was sharpened by my hand, and reminding the client that "*A sharpened pencil is a dangerous object; use with care.*"

CHAPTER 2:
ANATOMY OF THE #2 PENCIL

It is assumed the reader is already somewhat familiar with the #2 pencil. Let the remarks below serve only
to further refine his or her understanding in the context
of best sharpening practices.[1]

The typical #2 pencil is made of cedar. It is 7 ½" long,
with a wooden shaft measuring 6 ¾".[2]

UNSHARPENED PENCIL (SIDE VIEW)

SHARPENED PENCIL (SIDE VIEW)

a. THE TIP of the pencil is the marking surface farthest from the eraser.

b. THE POINT of the pencil, for the purposes of this
book, refers to the cone whose end is the pencil's tip and
whose base is the upper limit of the unshaped shaft. This

---

[1] Much of the information for this chapter was gleaned from Henry Petroski's
exhaustive, magisterial *The Pencil: A History of Design and Circumstance*
(New York: Alfred A. Knopf, 1989), a volume which belongs on every pencil
enthusiast's shelf. There are few questions about the history and engineering
of pencils whose answers cannot be found between its covers.

[2] The latter measurement refers only to the exposed length of the shaft; some
of the wood is hidden within the ferrule, which is clamped around it.

means the point is composed of exposed graphite *and* cedar. (Conservative readers may object to this nomenclature; I trust they will become convinced of its utility as our book unfolds.)

c. THE COLLAR TOP is the boundary between cedar and graphite.

d. THE COLLAR is that part of the point with no exposed graphite. If one thinks of the exposed graphite as a balancing visual analogue to the eraser, the collar serves as a visual analogue to the ferrule.

e. THE COLLAR BOTTOM is the boundary between the bottom of the cone and the top of the untooled shaft. (On hexagonal pencils, it is defined by scalloped edges where the shaft's planar surfaces taper into the exposed cedar point; cylindrical pencils feature no such scalloping along the collar bottom.)

f. THE SHAFT is the wood casing surrounding the graphite core. It is also known as the body of the pencil. For #2 pencils sold in the United States, it is most often hexagonal.

g. THE FERRULE is a crimped piece of metal connecting the shaft of the pencil to the eraser.

h. THE ERASER is a mystery.

A pencil's "lead" is actually made from a mixture of graphite, clay, and wax, with a bonding agent applied to seal it inside the wooden shaft.[3] This process was first

---

[3] Early graphite deposits were misidentified as lead, and the appellation stuck.

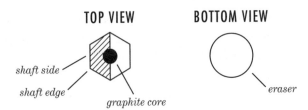

TOP VIEW   BOTTOM VIEW

shaft side

shaft edge

graphite core

eraser

developed by the Frenchman Nicolas-Jacques Conté in the late 18th century — an innovation that led to France's dominance of the pencil trade for years.

The amount of clay in the mixture determines the hardness of the lead — the more clay, the harder the point and the lighter the line. There is still no single international standard as to pencil-lead gradations. This book (and my business) focuses exclusively on #2 pencils, sometimes called HB pencils.

For years, I assumed pencils "got graphite" by having it injected into their hollow shafts. In fact, a close look at the unsharpened, or "raw" end of a pencil will usually reveal differences in color and/or grain of the opposing halves. This is because pencils are composed of two grooved pieces of cedar with a length of graphite sandwiched between them.[4]

EQUIVALENTS BETWEEN U.S. AND INTERNATIONAL PENCIL GRADATIONS, AS DEVELOPED BY CONTÉ AND THOREAU

U.S.	World
#1	B
#2	HB
#2 ½	F
#3	H
#4	2H

---

[4] Readers may be familiar with the phenomenon of alternating light and dark bands in a traditional ribbon of pencil shavings. This pleasing effect is the result of mismatched cedar halves in a single pencil.

Most #2 pencils are hexagonal. The design is justified by logistical and utilitarian concerns: Manufacturers realized the same piece of wood yielded more hexagonal shafts than cylindrical shafts; hexagonal pencils are less likely to roll off slanted drafting tables.[5]

You should always inspect a pencil before sharpening it. The early history of pencil production was marked by inconsistency of manufacture and outright fraud (some pencils' leads only extended a few inches into the shaft; by the time the user sharpened a pencil enough to realize the deceit, it was too late). In our own time, as more and more pencils are produced abroad with an eye on minimizing cost, we are beset with low-quality examples of the classic #2 pencil, and it behooves us to inspect them for any deficiencies that would render sharpening attempts futile.[6]

---

[5] Similarly, the flattened rectangular shaft of a carpenter's pencil makes it safe to deposit on a sharply sloped roof.

[6] Alas, the most common complaint about modern pencils concerns a shortcoming that cannot be easily ascertained by visual inspection alone: Poor-quality leads that break during sharpening, or upon application on the page. As the quality of a pencil's lead is determined by the quality of its component materials, it would be the gifted sharpener indeed who could appraise it solely by deconstructing it with his or her eyes!

However, there is one visual signifier that often predicts lead quality: The words "Made in USA" (or a European country) typically bespeaks a higher-quality pencil than "Made in China" (or "Made in Mexico"). This rule is not a product of jingoism (your author is American), but rather the cold facts of current pencil-manufacturing realities. Japanese pencils are also good.

A further point regarding lead-breakage: The single thing a pencil-user can do to increase the sorry likelihood of his or her lead breaking is dropping his or her pencil; the graphite core is vulnerable to internal shattering, which may not make itself known until the compromised section of graphite is revealed during the sharpening process. This is not to say we should coddle our pencils — they are, after all, tools to be used, and with vigor at that — but treating them with appropriate decorum cannot help but engender their finest possible utility.

The hexagonal shaft of the pencil must be straight, as bowing can lead to "shudder" in hand-crank sharpeners and irregular collars produced by pocket sharpeners. Rolling a pencil under your palm on a flat surface should reveal any bowing.

Make sure the graphite core is centered within the wooden shaft. An off-center lead will produce a point that gets progressively more difficult to sharpen evenly. Employing a pocketknife (see Chapter 4) will afford greater flexibility in pointing an errant core, but even still, the pencil user will have to moderate his or her pressure while applying that side of the point which runs closest to the edge of the shaft. Best to simply discard those pencils with cores that are more than 25% off-axis.[7]

The raw top of a new pencil should be free of paint. The iconic yellow (or black[8], or blue[9]) shaft of a pencil is colored by dipping it into a vat of paint; any paint that adheres to the raw end of a pencil bespeaks of irregularities in the finishing process, which, in turn, suggests irregularities in earlier stages of production — irregularities that indicate unfortunate compromise in matters more significant than aesthetics!

Remember: A pencil point enjoyed by the writer may not be suited for the draftsman; the ideal point for the standardized-test taker laboring in an over-lit classroom may not please the louche poet idling on a windswept

---

[7] Percentage is approximate and based on personal experience.

[8] I'm thinking of the infamous Palomino Blackwing.

[9] I'm thinking of German Faber-Castell pencils, which display the company's colors.

IRREGULAR PENCIL POINTS — A TAXONOMY

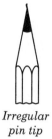   

Irregular pin tip　　*Irregular collar bottom*　　*"Throat" (exposed by irregular collar top)*　　*"Creeping collar"*　　*"Headless Horseman" / "Louis XVI"*

peak. No point can serve all needs. The unsharpened pencil is, in contrast, an idealized form.[10] Putting a point on a pencil — making it functional — is to lead it out of Plato's cave and into the noonday sun of utility. Of course, life outside a cave runs the risk of imperfection and frustration. But we must learn to live with these risks if we want enough oxygen to survive.

Let us now walk together into the sunlight.

---

[10] Most vintage-pencil collectors will not deign to include sharpened pencils in their collections.

CHAPTER 3:
WARM-UP EXERCISES

Sharpening pencils should be a pleasant activity that enriches the senses. (See Table 3.1.) However, it is a physical process,[1] and as such carries the risk of bodily harm. If you're in pain while sharpening a pencil, or racked with discomfort afterwards, you're probably doing something wrong: either gripping the pencil or the sharpener too tightly; sitting or standing in an awkward position; applying the blade of the sharpener to your body rather than the pencil; or (most common) failing to stretch and prepare your body before beginning the sharpening process.

In this respect, sharpening a pencil is no different from weightlifting, bungee jumping, or bull riding. All these activities require physical preparation and the constant monitoring of one's bodily integrity.

Take a few moments before each sharpening job to **make sure your body is comfortable, free of disease, and sufficiently stretched** to maintain the muscle control, flexibility, and range of motion necessary for pointing pencils.

Below we find a sampling of warm-up exercises that will increase the pleasure taken from sharpening pencils while decreasing the likelihood of injury and death.

---

[1] There is an exception to this claim; see Chapter 18.

What looks like a man repeatedly overcome with enthusiasm and celebrating with the traditional "thumbs up" gesture is actually a sober professional engaging in an important warm-up exercise before using a hand-crank sharpener that requires hand-stabilization of the pencil. (Hand-stabilization of a pencil can place strain on the thumb.) (See Chapter 10.)

Similarly, the reader is forgiven for assuming these photographs show an enraged business owner struggling to contain his desire to backhand a subordinate who has given offense. In fact, the event captured in these images is a happy one: The artisanal pencil sharpener stretches his deltoids in anticipation of a busy day's work!

If you plan on sharpening pencils while sitting at a desk or worktable, it is incumbent on you to **monitor your posture** and **sit with your abdominal muscles flexed** so as to reduce strain on your lower back. You should also **stretch your lower back** at the beginning and end of each day in your workshop, as well as before and after each individual sharpening job and in between any other activities.

You will find further utility in the above posture when it comes to using wall-mounted sharpeners. (See Chapter 15.)

Fully 95% of the body's movements while sharpening a pencil occur in the wrists and fingers, except for those movements located elsewhere, which range between 10% and 80% of other movements spanning 50% or 65% of the body. Your fingers are on the front lines of every traditional pencil-sharpening technique—it is said the secret motto of electric pencil sharpeners is: *"First their pencils, then their fingers"*—and must be up to the job. **Do not neglect your fingers** while warming up for an afternoon of work.

There are, famously, almost as many finger warm-up techniques as there are fingers, but I have found this exercise to be especially efficient and elegant:

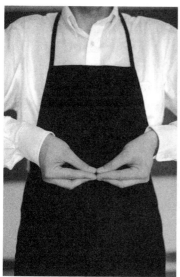 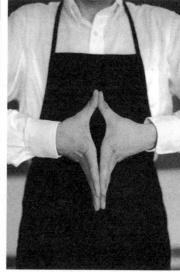

A profitable quarter-hour can be spent in the performance of this repeating gesture. Your rewards will be many; perhaps the most important will be fingers from which the cobwebs have been thoroughly shaken — fingers that are limber, strong, and primed for both pencil and blade.

Carpal-tunnel syndrome is as serious a threat for the pencil sharpener as it is for the guitarist or golfer, and stretching your wrists is a crucial component in any pre-sharpening warm-up ritual. **Take care not to overtax your wrists while warming them up.** An effective way to monitor wrist pain while doing this exercise is to watch yourself in a mirror — if you notice signs of discomfort in your face, you're probably straining your wrist.

As you develop your practice, make note of any sites of agony that reveal themselves during or after a job. Consult with a physician or yogi to develop a strategy for strengthening and otherwise conditioning those body parts. Each body is different, after all, and some of the more defective among us may need further regimens to ensure peak performance.

3.1: HOW SHARPENING PENCILS CAN ENRICH THE SENSES

Sense: SIGHT	The shape of a properly sharpened pencil can please the eyes
Sense: SMELL	The potpourri of graphite and cedar found in pencil shavings can please the nose
Sense: TOUCH	The smooth, unblemished cedar of a properly shaped pencil collar can please the fingertips
Sense: HEARING	The steady whisper of sharpener blades moving against the pencil shaft can please the ears
Sense: TASTE	The food you buy with your income from sharpening pencils can please the tongue

3.2: PARTS OF THE BODY THAT CAN BE DAMAGED AS A RESULT OF INCORRECT PENCIL SHARPENING TECHNIQUE

Fingers	Forearms	Shoulders
Palms	Throat	Neck
Wrists	Ears	Feet
Elbows	Lower back	Eyes

EQUIPMENT CHECKLIST:

- Whetstone
- Mineral spirits
- Emery board
- Sandpaper
- Pocketknife
- Pencils
- Additional pencils
  (for beginners)

WE SHALL BEGIN WITH THE OLDEST METHOD of sharpening a pencil. Long before the dawn of the hand-crank sharpener; centuries before the domesticated whine of the Boston electric; in the days when "pre-sharpened" pencils sold in flimsy plastic boxes were the stuff of fever-dreams, if a man wanted to ready a pencil for use, he reached for a knife.

In our age of abundance, when we are spoiled for choice with all manner of pencil-pointing technologies, what does it profit a man to take up this old tool? After all, compared to other pencil sharpeners, the knife carries the greatest risk of physical harm and the slimmest guarantee of a proper point — at least for the novice. Shouldn't we be content to let this centuries-old technique continue its lonely hobble towards irrelevance?

The happy fact of the matter is that sharpening a pencil with a straight blade (here, a pocketknife; other times, a box cutter) offers satisfaction and variety unavailable to other tools. In skilled hands, the humble pocketknife — that old wizard — can conjure as many pencil points as the human mind can picture.

It also behooves us to remember the adage that *"Whensoever a member of our modern world sharpens a pencil using a pocketknife, he or she moves forward and backward through time simultaneously"*: forward, insofar as the knife is deployed concurrently with the world's temporal flow and anticipates a future state of affairs (i.e., the sharpened point, itself suggesting astronomer Arthur Eddington's "arrow of time"); backward, as the persistent movements of the knife function as pistons in a nostalgia-engine which delivers its user to the distant past.

Indeed, when I tell people about my artisanal pencil sharpening business, I am often rewarded with their vivid memories of grandfathers, art teachers, or other beloved forebears sharpening pencils with pocketknives. Sharpening a pencil "the old-fashioned way" allows the modern enthusiast to reconnect with all those who have sharpened pencils in centuries past, and further sustains a rich tradition of pencil-pointing that would otherwise run the risk of disappearing entirely.

Addressing all the ways of applying pocketknife to pencil — and the points produced thereby — could fill a book, if not a library. For this chapter, it will suffice to provide a basic understanding of the tool and its technique. Readers are encouraged to take this chapter not as an exhaustive reckoning, but as a firm foundation upon which to build edifices of their own experience.

STEP ONE: OPENING THE POCKETKNIFE

Take up your pocketknife. Notice that it fits easily in one hand. The blade is hidden within its handle; it will make itself known soon enough.

Carefully open the blade of the pocketknife. The blade should open smoothly and quietly. It should be clean. Its base (or tang) should enjoy a snug fit within the handle, not subject to wobbling when pressure is applied anywhere on the blade.

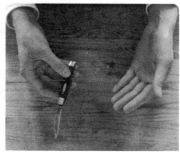

Here, then, is the pocketknife as you will use it: blade open, handle resting comfortable in the hand. (If you're having trouble distinguishing between the blade and the handle, ask a more experienced friend or relative for help.)

STEP TWO: PREPARING THE BLADE FOR USE

The cook in his kitchen, the bandit in his alley, and the hunter standing over his steaming game can all agree on one thing: **a dull blade is more dangerous than a sharp one**. A dull blade requires a superabundance of force in order to cut — which increases the risk of error, slippage and injury.

The knife in the hand of the pencil sharpener is no different from that wielded by our friends the cook, the bandit, and the hunter. It must be kept sharp. If you plan on making pocketknives part of your pencil-sharpening practice, you must learn to keep them in peak condition. A whetstone is the simplest tool for sharpening your pocketknife, and should travel as its constant companion.[1]

---

[1] Unfortunately, detailed instructions for sharpening knives using a whetstone are beyond the scope of this book. Suffice to say the key concepts are: lubrication with mineral spirits; a steady angle of 10–15 degrees; light pressure applied evenly to the blade; alternating sides of the blade with increasing frequency; switching from the whetstone's coarse surface to its finer surface to complete the sharpening process; the preferability of not being blind drunk.

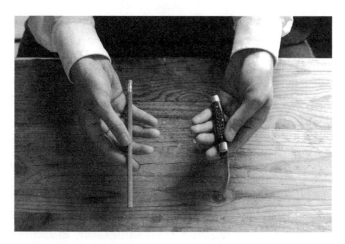

STEP THREE: "A TREAT IN EACH HAND"

After sharpening your knife, it's time to do the same to your pencil.

Holding the knife in your dominant hand, **use your other hand to pick up a pencil**. You should now have one object in each hand.

Unlike the other techniques discussed in this book, sharpening a pencil with a knife requires discrete movement from both elements, for which the user alone is responsible. You'll need to maintain a light, flexible grip on your knife as well as your pencil, and will likely find yourself using your fingers more than your palms.

4.1: PROPER LOCATION OF PENCIL AND POCKETKNIFE

| DOMINANT HAND: | Pocketknife |
| NON-DOMINANT HAND: | Pencil |

If you're worried about your ability to successfully manipulate pocketknife and pencil in concert, ask yourself this question: Are you able to navigate and consume a standard American dinner — soup, salad, meatloaf, dessert — using silverware? If so, your hand-eye coordination and fine motor skills are up to the task; it's a simple matter of setting off on the long and winding path to proficiency. (See page 49.)

STEP FOUR: CHOOSING YOUR COLLAR BOTTOM

Unlike most other sharpening techniques, in which blades engage the pencil's wood (and later, graphite) at an angle more or less parallel to the shaft, the pocketknife's blade is applied perpendicular to the pencil's shaft. It creates the pencil's point directly and from the bottom up, as opposed to obliquely and from the top down.

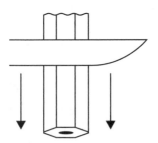

Pocketknife moves perpendicular to shaft

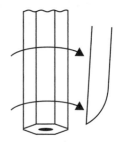

Pencil moves parallel/into pocket sharpener blade

This means you begin at the collar bottom, instead of ending at it. Before you make your first cut, therefore, you should determine how long you want your point to be, as

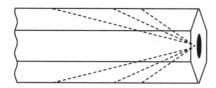

The longer your desired point, the further down the shaft you should begin, and the lower the angle of the blade relative to the pencil.

this will determine where to start, i.e. the location of your collar bottom.

For this demonstration I will produce a standard pencil point; this means my collar bottom should lie approximately ¾" from the top of the pencil.

Observant readers will protest that this photograph

shows my knife resting approximately 1 ½" from the top. Let me explain the inconsistency: When using a pocket-knife, **it's appropriate to give yourself a little breathing room**, especially the first few hundred times. After all, it's better to find yourself with too much space between the collar bottom and the hypothetical tip of the pencil than too little — in the first case, the tip can be easily shortened and the entire point re-shaped; in the second, you will likely have to start again from scratch, as it is difficult to graft additional wood and graphite onto a half-sharpened pencil.

STEP FIVE: THE FIRST INCISION

There is a lively debate among pocketknife pencil sharpeners as to whether it's preferable to place the blade flush with the plane of the pencil shaft, or to run it along the ridge between two sides. Both options have their appeal: Begin flush with the plane, and you can be sure of an even stroke. Begin on the ridge, and you may find the first stroke easier to make. **Experiment with both options before making a public declaration of your preference.**

In this photograph, we see the knife blade attacking the ridge. The cutting angle is low, due to the length of point desired (remember, the longer the point, the lower the angle of incision) and the simple reality that the first incisions need only remove the finished wood from the exterior of the pencil. There's no need to "strike oil" at the outset. A sharp knife in a patient hand will get the job done.

RELATIVE DIFFICULTY OF KNIFE-BASED ACTIVITIES FROM EASIEST TO MOST DIFFICULT, WITH SHARPENING A PENCIL REPRESENTING THE MEDIAN

If you can REACH FOR A KNIFE
 then you can PICK UP A KNIFE
If you can PICK UP A KNIFE
 then you can DIP A KNIFE IN A BATHTUB
If you can DIP A KNIFE IN A BATHTUB
 then you can SMEAR JELLY WITH A KNIFE
If you can SMEAR JELLY WITH A KNIFE then you
 can CUT A LOAF OF BREAD WITH A BREAD KNIFE
If you can CUT A LOAF OF BREAD WITH A BREAD KNIFE
 then you can CUT A STEAK WITH A STEAK KNIFE
If you can CUT A STEAK WITH A STEAK KNIFE then you can
 CARVE A TURKEY WITH A CARVING KNIFE
If you can CARVE A TURKEY WITH A CARVING KNIFE
 then you can CARVE A TOTEM POLE WITH A CHAINSAW
If you can CARVE A TOTEM POLE WITH A CHAINSAW then
 you can SHARPEN A PENCIL WITH A POCKETKNIFE
If you can SHARPEN A PENCIL WITH A POCKETKNIFE
 then you can WHITTLE A DUCK WITH A POCKETKNIFE
If you can WHITTLE A DUCK WITH A POCKETKNIFE then
 you can SHAVE A THREAD WITH A STRAIGHT RAZOR
If you can SHAVE A THREAD WITH A STRAIGHT RAZOR
 then you can REMOVE A CORNEA WITH A SCALPEL
If you can REMOVE A CORNEA WITH A SCALPEL then you
 can MAKE A LOT OF MONEY
If you can MAKE A LOT OF MONEY then you can HAVE AN
 AFFAIR WITH YOUR SECRETARY
If you can HAVE AN AFFAIR WITH YOUR SECRETARY
 then you can BE BLACKMAILED
If you can BE BLACKMAILED
 then you can IMAGINE COMMITTING A CRIME
If you can IMAGINE COMMITTING A CRIME
 then you can REACH FOR A KNIFE

Use the thumb of your "pencil hand" to push the knife forward along the shaft. It's one of the ironies of this technique that the hand holding the knife will be only minimally involved in its propulsion.

I prefer to work opposite sides of the shaft in sequence, to maintain conical symmetry.

STEP SIX: REVEALING AND SHAPING THE CEDAR

After you remove the painted outer surface of the pencil shaft, the unfinished cedar will take the knife easily. **Continue shaping your pencil point,** beginning each stroke at the collar bottom you established earlier.

One risk associated with the pocketknife is cutting too deeply into the pencil shaft and hitting the graphite core. The inexperienced pencil-pocketknifer will quickly come to know the frustration of gouging the graphite below the desired location of the pencil tip. As well as weakening the graphite, whenever these marks catch the light they blaze as unfortunate testaments to overzealousness, like divots on a golf green.[2] It's best to err on the side of

---

[2] Similarly, the constellation of acne scars on my temples memorialize an adolescence defined by too much passion; my complexion has much improved since I jettisoned all emotion and declared myself a psychological eunuch with nothing to live for beyond pencils.

caution, not digging too aggressively into the pencil.

In this photograph we see the cedar-removal process nearly complete. The graphite core awaits the first hint of spring within its cocoon.

STEP SEVEN: EXPOSING THE GRAPHITE

Continue shaving away the wood of the pencil shaft until the core is exposed. **Turn the pencil in your hand** to confirm that no cedar tendrils still cling to the graphite, as they could interfere with final shaping of the point. If you do find a stray sliver of wood extending from the collar top, you can remove it with a delicate application of the knife or emery board.

Now is also a good time to even out your collar

bottom, should you see fit. I rarely touch up my collar bottoms after using a knife; one of the aesthetic pleasures of the technique, after all, is the rustic quality it lends a pencil — and an uneven collar bottom is a sure sign that a #2 did not come to its point via electric sharpener (see Chapter 13).

This is not to say that we should take imperfection as our goal. One of the dysfunctions of our age is the conflation of shoddiness with authenticity, and we must resist this confusion in our practice — especially in those circumstances where sloppy craftsmanship could diminish a pencil's utility. Having said that, collar bottoms exhibiting uneven borders between finished and unfinished cedar don't pose a threat to functionality and may be left as they are found.

The graphite is exposed.

If you're satisfied with your work so far, take a minute to drink a glass of water and **celebrate your accomplishment**: The wood of the pencil has been shaped; it may now serve as the "launching pad" for your graphite pencil point.

STEP EIGHT: FINISHING THE GRAPHITE

Now that the graphite is exposed and ready for shaping we find ourselves with multiple options. If your pocketknife is the only tool available, you may finish the point by shaving it with the knife blade angled away from the top of the pencil.

Don't make the mistake of shaving the graphite with the knife blade facing forward: as mentioned above, the risk of gouging into the graphite is too great, and would require further abrasion to maintain consistency. (Such a perpetual **"escalation of abrasion"** is one of the most frustrating dysfunctions associated with the use of a pocketknife — anyone who has tried to cut his own sideburns will be familiar with this agony — and has led many a novice to throw away their knife in despair.)

A safer bet is to shape the graphite with high-grit sandpaper or an emery board.

If you desire a relatively clean point, in which the graphite flows seamlessly from its cedar sheath, be sure to **follow the angle of the exposed wood** while shaping the point. (You may find it easier to do so if you position the sandpaper over the edge of a table and engage the graphite along the top edge, leaving the cedar untouched.)

Congratulations! You have sharpened a pencil using a pocketknife, and now stand as heir to a proud tradition. Don't worry if your first attempts look less like functional pencils and more like beaver-savaged branches; after a few weeks of practice you will find your stockpile of intuitions and sense memories increasing, and, as the anxiety of the neophyte falls away, you will enjoy greater confidence and ability each time you take your knife in hand and apply it to an unsharpened pencil. (Alternately, you can 'hone' your knife-skills using a Little Shaver-style sharpener.) (See page 103.)

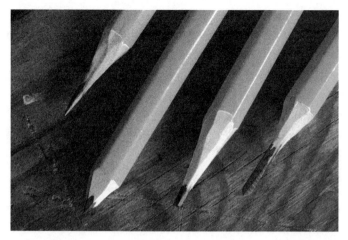

Four points are submitted for review, each of which was produced by a pocketknife. Of course, these represent only a fraction of the styles that can be created by a skilled hand — readers should try replicating each of these points before branching off into their own distributaries of exploration.

On the left we see a long, elegant point with a shapely collar that curves as it approaches the graphite. (This effect is achieved by lowering the blade's angle in a scooping motion as it approaches the top of the pencil.) The graphite was finished using sandpaper; its form is smooth and muscular. This pencil recommends itself to the architect, graphic designer, or any other professional whose vocation entails a narrow line and an abundance of vanity. I trust you'll agree it also holds its own as an object for display. (I call this point "the poor man's El Casco;" the reference will become clear in Chapter 10.)

Our stubby friend, second from the left, was the quickest point to produce, and the only one that didn't require a separate finishing stage for the exposed graphite. As you can see, the graphite and wood form a single plane — a sure sign that the point was produced via rapid cuts from the collar bottom toward the top of the pencil, cutting wood and graphite simultaneously. (This calls for an extremely sharp knife.) Indeed, this "quick and dirty" point can be produced in a matter of seconds; its savage utility makes it a favorite of the harried woodworker or housewife — though its minimal graphite exposure will require constant maintenance and renewal, and as such is not recommended for languid poets of the Romantic school.

Third from the left we find an unusual point, a provocative showcase of elegance and brute force. (Readers are invited to join me in referring to this point as "the Lamborghini Countach," in honor of the legendary Italian sports car whose image occupied my every waking moment from ages twelve to fourteen.) This example is remarkable for the low ratio of graphite to exposed cedar: approximately 1:5. This ensures a point that can withstand greater than normal pressure in application, as most of its graphite core remains buttressed by wood. The flattened tip further suggests its use for intense, heavy mark-making — it is easy to imagine this pencil in the calloused hands of the contractor, the butcher, or the shack-dwelling megalomaniac with ideas to share.

The complicated point on the far right offers no less

than four discrete surfaces for mark-making. It is ideal for the artist who works quickly and intuitively, and desires "many pencils in one." Its resemblance to the beveled blade of a broadsword promises its inclusion in many a dungeon master's Trapper Keeper.

Now that you have some sense of the variety of pencil points available to the skilled pocketknife user, I encourage you to use the space below to sketch out some "fantasy pencil points" you'd like to try making.

In plotting your pointing strategy, ask yourself how collar-bottom location, blade angle, stroke length, finishing process, and other technical considerations will inform your creation. (The dotted lines represent the graphite core; keep this in mind while plotting your masterpiece!)

FANTASY PENCIL POINTS—AN EXERCISE

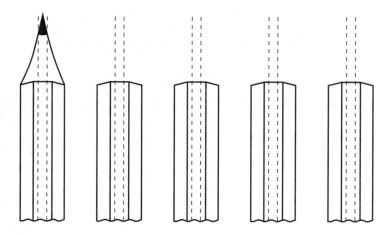

CHAPTER 5:
USING A SINGLE-BLADE POCKET SHARPENER

EQUIPMENT CHECKLIST:

- Emery board
- Toothpick
- Magnifying lenses
- Tweezers
- Bag
- Single-blade pocket sharpener
- Pencil (not pictured)

OF ALL PENCIL-SHARPENERS, THE HUMBLE single-blade pocket model is perhaps the most ubiquitous. That doesn't mean our little friend is easy to master. On the contrary, its unassuming appearance gives no hint of the potential frustrations, pitfalls, brambles, dead-ends, and heartbreaks that lie within.

I approach every use of a pocket sharpener with guarded optimism. As far as I'm concerned, it offers the most intimate encounter with a pencil. It's my favorite sharpening technique precisely because, like all intimate encounters, its ideal outcome is so obvious yet its practical application is so fraught with peril.

STEP ONE: INSPECTING AND CLEANING THE SHARPENER

Before beginning the sharpening process, **do a quick visual inspection of the sharpener**. The casing should be free of cracks and blemishes. The blade should be properly aligned relative to the body of the sharpener and free of rust, blood, or other elements that could compromise the blade's motion across the surface of the pencil.

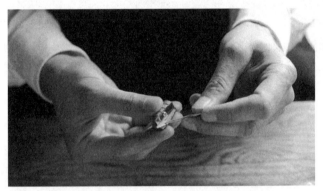

If wood shavings or graphite residue from previous use are lodged against the blade, remove them by gently inserting a wooden toothpick between the blade and the opposite plane. Pull the toothpick towards the sharpener's entrance hole, collecting debris as you go.

STEP TWO: PLACING THE TOOL IN HAND

Hold the sharpener in your non-dominant hand so it rests comfortably between your thumb and index finger. Apply your middle finger to the body of the sharpener so as to stabilize it during the sharpening process. The

blade should be face-up and visible throughout the process, as you will be monitoring its contact with the pencil as well as the unfurling of shavings.

Hold the pencil in your dominant hand. You will be rotating the pencil, not the sharpener. The sharpener should remain stationary throughout the process, barring extreme circumstances.[1]

STEP THREE: ENGAGEMENT

Begin rotating the pencil inside the body of the sharpener so the blade is engaging with the shaft of the pencil. For left-handers, this means a clockwise rotation.[2] Maintain steady, moderate pressure along the shaft as you guide it towards the forward end of the sharpener.

---

[1] One of the kinetic differences between a single-blade sharpener and a hand-crank sharpener is the movement of the pencil relative to the tool — a hand-crank sharpener usually requires the pencil to remain motionless as the sharpener's blade(s) rotate around it.

[2] Further research is required to determine what it means for right-handers, and is beyond the scope of this book.

STEP FOUR: MONITORING THE SHAVINGS' EGRESS

Many of my clients request the use of a single-blade hand sharpener because of the iconic, scalloped ribbon of shavings it produces. (Sometimes called "the apple-peel effect" or "M'lady's ruffled skirt abandoned on the floor in the throes of our love-making.") Although you may be tempted to focus exclusively on the pencil point, attention must be paid to the merry byproduct of your labor.

As pencil shavings begin to curl out of the sharpener, **turn the sharpener away from you** so the shavings fall to the side and don't obscure the blade. Do not allow the shavings to collect in your palm. Shavings should unfurl completely, lest they jam the sharpener.

If shavings are reluctant to leave the sharpener's planar orifice, a gentle tug will release them from its grasp. Place them on a flat surface and return to the task at hand.

STEP FIVE: CHECKING IN WITH YOUR PENCIL

After some time you should notice the pencil point beginning to take shape and feel the sharpener engaging the newly exposed graphite, which will offer less resistance than the wood. (See Table 5.1.) This typically happens after thirteen to fifteen rotations. **Now is the time to pay especially close attention** to your pencil's progress. You may be tempted to remove the pencil and test its point

after one or two further rotations. Resist the temptation a bit longer — approximately two more rotations, if not one additional rotation, or even a further, final rotation.

Remove the pencil and look at it.

If the pencil is still not sharp enough, engage the sharpener in one or two additional rotations. **Avoid a third rotation**, a.k.a. "the Devil's Dance."

STEP SIX: "A CLOSER LOOK"

Use your magnifying spectacles to **search the pencil point for irregularities**. In this photograph, we see a ragged edge to the collar at the site where the sharpening process was concluded. This begs for correction.

5.1: TYPICAL LENGTH OF PENCIL AFTER EACH FULL ROTATION IN SINGLE-BLADE POCKET SHARPENER, BLADE LENGTH = $^{29}/_{32}$ INCH, MODERATE PRESSURE APPLIED

Original pencil length (zero rotations):	7½ inches
After one rotation:	7½ inches
After two rotations:	7½ inches
After three rotations:	7½ inches
After four rotations:	7½ inches
After five rotations:	7½ inches
After six rotations:	7½ inches (sharpener is still shaving wood; no graphite exposure)
After seven rotations:	7½ inches
After eight rotations:	7½ inches
After nine rotations:	7½ inches
After ten rotations:	7½ inches
After eleven rotations:	7½ inches
After twelve rotations:	7½ inches
After thirteen rotations:	7½ inches (360 degrees of graphite exposed)
After fourteen rotations:	7½ inches
After fifteen rotations:	7½ inches (noticeable amount of graphite swarf along with wood shavings)
After sixteen rotations:	7½ inches (turning pencil inside sharpener notably easier due to reduced contact of blade against wood)
After seventeen rotations:	7$^{15}/_{32}$ inches (could be plausibly identified as "sharp")
After eighteen rotations:	7$^{7}/_{16}$ inches
After nineteen rotations:	7$^{7}/_{16}$ inches
After twenty rotations:	7$^{3}/_{8}$ inches
After twenty-one rotations:	7$^{11}/_{32}$ inches (good place to stop; further sharpening increases the risk of breaking the pencil's tip)
After twenty-two rotations:	7$^{11}/_{32}$ inches
After twenty-three rotations:	7¼ inches (tip broke off)
After twenty-four rotations:	7$^{7}/_{32}$ inches
After twenty-five rotations:	7$^{7}/_{32}$ inches (project abandoned)

STEP SEVEN: CORRECTING THE COLLAR

You can further improve the pencil by removing the raised edge where the blade last encountered the collar. **Smooth the collar** with an emery board, taking care not to flatten its conical surface. A light touch is key.

After smoothing the collar, **clean any graphite residue** with a cotton handkerchief or rag. Make sure not to damage the graphite and the tip!

STEP EIGHT: "BAGGING THE BIG GAME"

At the end of the sharpening process, you must attend to the shavings. They are part of the pencil and, as such, should be returned to their rightful owner.

A bag of clean shavings, besides looking delightful, should put to rest any concerns your clients may have about your technique: that you used an electric sharpener  instead of a hand-sharpener; that you hoard shavings for your personal use; that the "pencil" is a plastic simulacrum; that you passed the shavings through your body before returning them, etc.

Using tweezers, **carefully place the shavings in a bag**. Label the shavings and pencil according to your preferred indexing system.

STEP NINE: REVIEWING YOUR HANDIWORK

This step can be emotionally wrenching, but it's required if you hope to improve your practice. Taking a long look at your finished pencil is an opportunity for reflection and renewal.

While reviewing your handiwork, ask yourself the following questions:

1. **How closely does the pencil point correspond to your desired outcome?** Is it sharper or duller than you wanted? If the former is the case, review the rotations recorded for this job in your log book and try one or two fewer rotations on your next pencil; if the latter, add rotations — keeping in mind that most pocket sharpeners lack a physical bulwark against over-sharpening, thereby risking the production of an irregular "pin-tip" which may break at the slightest pressure and leave the point further compromised.

2. **Is the collar-top consistent around the point and flush with the graphite?** Are there dips or scoops in the wood you didn't intend?[3] (These issues may have more to do with the quality of your pencil than your abilities; lesser pencils may have a loose or otherwise imperfect bond between the graphite core and the wooden shaft.)

---

[3] A single dramatic scoop in the collar-top is not necessarily a blemish; it may lend an air of sophistication or erotic *frisson* to an otherwise unremarkable pencil point. (One is reminded of the eighteenth-century courtesan's practice of adding a "beauty mark" to an otherwise perfect face.)

3. **Does the exposed graphite show signs of irregularity?** Are there divots associated with inconsistent pressure applied during the sharpening process? Again, an inferior pencil may be the culprit, as pencil-core production involves a delicate balance of graphite, clay, and wax — which may, in lesser models, be less than uniform throughout the core. Nevertheless, too much rotational torque during the sharpening process may gouge the graphite and leave a twisting "ghost image" of the sharpener blade.

The photo above exhibits several imperfections in a pencil point produced by a single-blade pocket sharpener. See if you can identify them, and consider how they could be reduced or eliminated in future jobs.

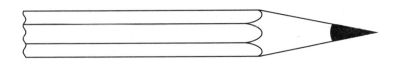

This illustration shows an ideal pencil point produced by a single-blade pocket sharpener. The collar's height stands at ½ inch, roughly equal to the length of the blade less the exposed graphite. The collar-bottom runs parallel to the ferrule and eraser, perpendicular to the edges of the shaft. The collar-top is uniform and parallel to the collar bottom; there is no gap between the wood and the graphite. The point is consistent and smooth, showing no mark of the blade. The tip is solid yet sharp; there is no "pin tip" waiting to shatter.

This pencil point could be usefully employed by the general-interest user. It offers hours of stable, uniform graphite exposure for writing, arithmetic, or doodling. Highly recommended for the layperson.

CHAPTER 6:
PROTECTING YOUR PENCIL POINT

If a pencil you've sharpened is not going to be used immediately, you should protect its point. I always carry a coil of $\frac{3}{8}$" × $\frac{1}{4}$" vinyl tubing in my tool kit for this purpose. (You can find such tubing in the plumbing section of your local hardware store.) Taking a few minutes to ensure the safety of a pencil point is a simple investment whose dividends include peace of mind, economy of effort, and insurance against heartache.

Woe betide the pencil sharpener who fails to safeguard his creation!

Needless to say, the piece of tubing must be long enough to cover the entire point, leaving none of the graphite exposed; it should also extend far enough beyond the tip to stabilize the pencil against the interior of a display tube's cap.

If you're unsure how long your piece of tubing should be, **place the pencil and display tube beside it** for comparison before making the incision. Although it may seem easiest to fit the pencil inside the tubing before cutting it to size, I don't recommend this strategy, as you may accidentally break the point while cutting through the vinyl.

Once you've calculated the proper length, **cut the tubing.**

The transformation is complete: What was once a humble piece of vinyl tubing is now a protective sheath tasked with preserving your pencil point against breakage.

Carefully place the protective sheath over the pencil point. It should fit snugly on the shaft of the pencil. Remember that the farther you push the sheath down the pencil shaft, the more difficult it will be to remove without risking damage to the point. There's no need for the sheath to extend more than ⅛ inch down the shaft.

With the point now protected, the pencil is ready to be fitted inside its display tube for shipping[1], or handed directly to the client for later use.

As long as it remains sheathed in vinyl and protected by its display tube, your pencil point will remain sharp for centuries. It will maintain its shape at any altitude, in large and small rooms alike.

For this we must thank our vinyl tubing.

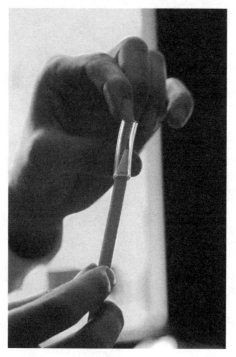

---

[1] To ensure the pencil doesn't fall out of the display tube, place a cap on each end.

CHAPTER 7:
USING A SINGLE-BURR
HAND-CRANK SHARPENER

EQUIPMENT CHECKLIST:
- Toothbrush
- Single-burr hand-crank sharpener
- Pencil
- Clamp or stable surface

THE MODERN HAND-CRANK PENCIL SHARPENER'S familiar morphology belies an alien tradition. As this method of pencil pointing wormed its way into the iconography of modern life, it left in its wake a viscous trail of engineering and experimentation that would leave today's user agog, if not aghast. (See page 87.)

Today's hand-crank sharpeners, regardless of

manufacturer, have converged on a more-or-less standard configuration: the sharpener's handle is connected to a planetary gear in which one or two cylinder blades, or burrs, rotate while circling and shaping the pencil. The shape of the point is determined by the angle of the burr relative to the pencil shaft.

In the single-burr iteration, the pencil rests inside a shaping sleeve with an opening exposed to the cylinder blade. As the handle is cranked, the shaping sleeve spins around the pencil, allowing the blade access to all sides of the shaft.

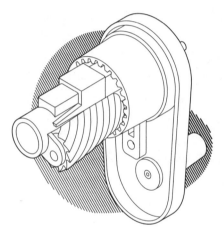

Single-burr sharpening mechanism

This chapter shall take as its focus the single-burr iteration of the hand-crank sharpener. Once the user feels comfortable with this device, both its theoretical under-pinning and its practical application, he or she can move on to grappling with its more sophisticated double-burr cousin.

STEP ONE: MAKING YOURS A CLEAN MACHINE

The first rule of hand-crank pencil sharpeners is: **"A clean machine is a mean machine."**

Unless the sharpener is "fresh from the box," you should begin by examining the cylinder blade. Most single-burr hand-crank sharpeners allow visual and physical assessment of the blade via the shavings drawer — remove the drawer and look upwards, into the device's interior. (Remember to replace the shavings drawer before use!)

Use a soft-bristle toothbrush to clean the blade.

If you'd like a closer look at the blade and gears, removing the sharpening mechanism from the housing is usually a simple affair. I recommend this deeper level of examination for first-time users, as it goes a long way towards demystifying the engineering of the hand-crank sharpener — if you've always wondered why the CARL Angel-5 produces a longer point than the Dahle 166, removing and comparing the devices' sharpening components will reveal a difference in cylinder-blade angles that should settle the issue definitively.

Once you are assured the pencil sharpener is clean and running smoothly, it is time to put it to use.

STEP TWO: MINIMIZING TRUNCATION

Many hand-crank sharpeners offer dialed adjustment for different points via the extension or retraction of a tiny slat within the shaping sleeve. The slat limits how deeply the pencil is allowed to intrude within the sleeve while being sharpened by the circling blade.[1]

Attentive readers will conclude that this system doesn't actually affect the conical shape of the cedar point, but rather the amount of graphite extending from the collar top before being cut off: "The adjustment is one of truncation," they cry, "and as such, offers a flat tip at every setting except the one which allows for a true tip!"

They are correct, and should be commended for their acuity and enthusiasm.

If your device offers different pencil points, **set the dial for the sharpest setting before beginning**.

STEP THREE: PREPARING TO SECURE THE PENCIL

Unlike the single-blade pocket sharpener or the pocketknife, the single-burr hand-crank sharpener does not require that the pencil turn against the cutting mechanism, either continuously (like the pocket sharpener) or

---

[1] Most hand-crank sharpeners — even those without adjustment dials — feature a stopper at the far end of the shaping sleeve to prevent over-sharpening. Although this eliminates the occurrence of irregular pin-tips, it may entail a separate finishing process for those who want a perfect point.

in discrete rotations (like the pocket knife). Heavy-handed daredevils may attempt to rotate the pencil against the cylinder blade, but the effect on the point is negligible, and certainly not worth the increased risk of cedar scuffing, graphite breakage, or other damage.

Make no mistake: This technique requires a stable pencil, and said stabilization will be provided by the sharpener. Whether that sharpener is the man or his machine is another matter.

Please understand, some hand-crank pencil sharpeners feature a spring-loaded intake mechanism that stabilizes the pencil, while others offer no such appendage, leaving the job of pencil-stabilization to the sharpener operator's hand.

The correct method of hand-stabilizing a pencil in a hand-crank pencil sharpener will be addressed in Chapter 10; in this chapter we will focus on those devices with extendable stabilizing faceplates.[2]

There are two intake mechanisms common to the hand-crank sharpener, distinguished by the location of their aperture controls. (The aperture secures the pencil shaft within retractable teeth.) Some machines, like the Swordfish Scholar, the Classroom Friendly Supplies sharpener, and the ELM-148, have two tabs on top of the extendable faceplate; as the tabs are brought together, the aperture opens.

---

[2] The terms "spring-loaded intake mechanism" and "extendable stabilizing faceplate" will be used interchangeably in this chapter; both refer to the pencil sharpener's spring-loaded, extendable intake stabilizing faceplate mechanism.

The sharpener pictured here (the Dahle 166) finds its aperture operated by a button on the body of the sharpener.

Be aware that the serrated teeth of intake apertures may leave indentations where they grab the pencil. If you are sharpening a pencil for display, such

8.1: PHRASES IN PROMOTIONAL/INSTRUCTIONAL COPY
FOR HAND-CRANK SHARPENERS THAT SHOULD MAKE
ONE WARY OF THEIR PURCHASE AND/OR USE

Does not work on pencils

The manufacturer shall not be held liable for

Usually does not smell like an old lady's foot

Elevate the bleeding appendage

Sustained ringing in the ears

Tetanus shot

Does not necessarily mean your finger will fall off

Risk of blindness

A further series of anal suppositories

imperfections may dissuade you from using a spring-loaded intake. You may enjoy better results with a hand-crank sharpener in which you hold and guide the pencil.

After watching the jaws of the aperture open in hungry anticipation, one may be tempted to

Our little friend is hungry.

insert the pencil, but this would be folly — until the faceplate is pulled away from the body of the sharpener, there will be no tension moving the pencil into the sharpening mechanism.

Create the appropriate tension by drawing the faceplate away from the body of the sharpener. You should feel the strength of the faceplate's springs as they struggle against your fingers to pull the faceplate back to its resting position.

"Don't worry, little springs," you may whisper, "you shall have your rest — but first I have a treat for you to draw into the body of the sharpening mechanism."

Sure enough, with its aperture open and its faceplate extended, the sharpener is finally ready to receive its pencil.

Let us tarry no longer!

STEP FOUR: INSERTING AND SECURING THE PENCIL

Place the pencil through the toothed aperture and into the entrance hole of the sharpener's body. Gently remove your finger from the aperture's release button and allow the teeth to bite into the shaft. You should feel the top of the pencil fitting snugly inside the shaping sleeve as the pencil is stabilized parallel to the surface on which the sharpener rests.

Take a moment to admire your handiwork: You have placed a pencil in a single-burr hand-crank sharpener!

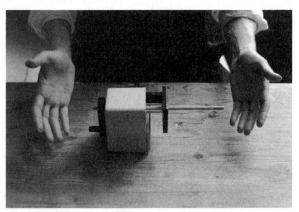

"Look on my works, ye mighty, and despair!"

STEP FIVE: EMPLOYING A CLAMP OR ADMINISTERING DOWNWARD PRESSURE TO STABILIZE THE SHARPENER

Needless to say, the body of the sharpener should not move during the pencil-pointing process. Unexpected or radical movements could surprise the user and lead to a "handle spasm" in which the hand-crank is jerked or its smooth rotation is otherwise interrupted, which could damage the pencil held in the device's interior or interrupt one's counting of handle rotations.[3]

Like many hand-crank sharpeners, the model pictured here ships with a removable clamp. I never use clamps, as I enjoy the flexibility of being able to reposition the device to maximize natural light exposure. Since the pencil is secured via the intake mechanism, I can use my free hand to stabilize the sharpener from above.

If you are using a single-burr hand-crank sharpener that doesn't feature a spring-loaded intake mechanism, your non-cranking hand must guide the pencil into the device — which means, of course, that you will need to use a clamp or suction base to maintain stability of the device. Some users go so far as to glue their sharpener to the table top!

But enough of these nightmare scenarios: Let us return to the device before us.

Place your hand on top of the sharpener and press down.

There are now two forces acting upon the body of the sharpener: The downward pressure administered by your hand, and

---

[3] Remember, for this and every other form of pencil sharpening, the rule: *Unexpected movement leads to loss of control; loss of control leads to inconsistency of blade engagement; inconsistency of blade engagement leads to a compromised pencil point.*

an opposite force being applied from the surface on which the sharpener rests.

This simple physics lesson should underscore the importance of resting your sharpener on a stable platform; a weak or wobbly table may not be able to withstand the downward pressure of your hand.

STEP SIX: TURNING THE HANDLE
TO SHARPEN THE PENCIL

It is time to begin turning the handle of the sharpener. **Rotate the crank evenly at a moderate speed.** It should take approximately ⅕ of a second to make a full rotation; your hand should be moving about as quickly as it does while stirring soup. If the burr cylinder is sharp, you will experience only slight resistance while shaping the pencil.

As you turn the handle, **make sure the pencil is drawn further into the sharpener** by the spring-loaded intake mechanism, as this indicates the top is being shortened, i.e. shaped.

After fifteen handle-rotations you should feel the resistance give way as the point comes closer to completion and the blades find less wood and graphite to engage. When the handle turns as easily as it did before the pencil's insertion, and the pencil is no longer moving into the sharpener, and the sharpener's cacophony has given way to silence, it is safe to release the pencil from the aperture for inspection.

Here we see a point typical of a medium-quality single-burr hand-crank sharpener. The collar-bottom is uniform, with no visible chafing. The exposed cedar of the collar is smooth and even around the cone, showing no irritation or roughness. The collar-top betrays slight inconsistencies in the border with the graphite, but none that will compromise the user experience.

The ratio of exposed graphite to cedar is approximately 1:3, indicating a stable fulcrum capable of withstanding moderate pressure. A point with this ratio is appropriate for drafting a letter of complaint or any other dispatch in which the user's emotion may lead to a slight increase in pressure applied to the pencil in its journey across the page.

Looking closely, we notice a slight irregularity in the reflected light on the graphite, approximately halfway between the collar-top and the tip. This is likely due to the graphite composition itself, rather than the sharpener — though it behooves one to record such imperfections in one's log, as repeated irregularities may indicate a flaw in the device rather than the pencil.

The stopper has done its job: far from being oversharpened, the tip of the pencil is flat and perpendicular to the pencil shaft, ensuring even wear as long as the pencil is rotated during deployment. Those who desire a sharper point can finish the job with construction paper or high-grit sandpaper.

In summary, this is a handsome, functional point that doesn't call attention to itself — perfect for middle-management professionals and khaki-trouser enthusiasts. Not recommended for drafting or engineering work, as the point is relatively stocky and as such offers limited visibility-of-line at some angles.

Its ease of production further recommends this point (and the tool which shaped it) to the non-specialist, especially in cases when many pencils must be sharpened in one sitting.

All in all, a pleasant (if un-extraordinary) experience awaits those who take this pencil in hand.

Renewing a point with a hand-crank sharpener is recommended only after moderate use, as the cylinder blade may have difficulty finding purchase on a point that retains more than 80% of its original shape. [4]

---

[4] Percentage is approximate and based on personal experience.

ANTIQUE PENCIL SHARPENERS: A REVERIE

An early example of hand-crank sharpener technology, the Planetary Pencil Pointer (ca. 1896) retains its power to astonish thanks to its exposed gears and iron construction. Using this device affords satisfactions no doubt familiar to certain participants in the Medieval Inquisition.

Your author's favorite antique pencil sharpener dealer calls the Roneo Model 6 (ca. 1910) "a very distinctive and unique pencil sharpener and an absolute must for any serious pencil sharpener collection," a verdict no sane man dare contradict. The massive base is actually a shavings receptacle, recommending this device for high-volume jobs. The Roneo is notable for being one of the first sharpeners to feature an extendable faceplate mechanism. It is further notable for looking unbelievable.

EQUIPMENT CHECKLIST:
- Multiple-hole sharpener
- Dust mask (optional)
- Pencil

ANY POCKET SHARPENER WITH TWO HOLES IS, technically, a multiple-hole sharpener — but not necessarily a *multiple-stage* multiple-hole sharpener of the type within this chapter's purview. A pocket sharpener with one #2-sized hole (⁵⁄₁₆") and a second, larger hole is actually a "two-in-one" device, with the larger hole designed for oversized color pencils. As this book deals exclusively with #2 pencils, such a device is of no interest to us; any that cross your path may be freely discarded.

The multi-stage, multi-hole pocket sharpener offers more control in shaping the pencil point than the single-blade pocket sharpener. The single-blade device allows minimal flexibility, insofar as cedar and graphite are simultaneously honed by one blade at a set angle. The device covered in this chapter breaks the sharpening process into two discrete stages; once the graphite is exposed, the user decides how much of it to shape and with what intensity by calibrating its contact with the second blade.

Needless to say, taking up the multi-hole sharpener is recommended only to those users who have mastered the single-hole, single-blade sharpener discussed in Chapter 5.

STEP ONE: (FIRST STAGE) SHAPING THE COLLAR AND EXPOSING THE GRAPHITE CORE

(It is assumed the reader understands that cleaning the blades of debris is required before using the sharpener; refer to Chapter 5 if need be.)

As we are presented with two holes, we must choose our first with care. Fortunately, most devices (like the KUM/Palomino Long Point sharpener) clearly label the proper sequence of holes; others, like the Alvin Magnesium Triple Hole pencil sharpener (used for this chapter)[1]

---

[1] The Alvin, as its full name implies, offers a third hole which is used in isolation, as a single-blade pocket sharpener. This hole will not be used in this chapter.

indicate the proper sequence via their engineering — the hole with the longer blade is used first, with the second, shorter blade reserved for the finishing process (see below).

Insert the pencil into the first hole as if you were using a single-blade pocket sharpener, observing the same principles: sharpener stabilized against the thumb and forefinger; moderate forward and torsional pressure applied to the pencil shaft; steady rotation of the shaft against the blade; and close observation of the proceedings, with a mandate to abort the process in the event of catastrophe.

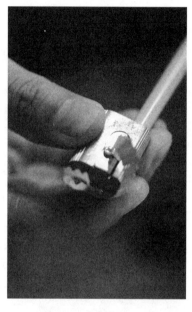

This initial process will feel, in its opening moments, identical to that associated with the single-blade pocket sharpener. The pencil shaft will move deeper into the body of the sharpener; shavings will flow from the slit between the blade and the sharpener casing; the odor of cedar will tickle the nostrils.

Continue until you are rewarded with the sight of unshaped graphite moving through the sharpener's body and into the open air.

STEP TWO: MONITORING THE EGRESS, NOT OF SHAVINGS, BUT OF THE GRAPHITE CORE ITSELF!

There is nothing quite so amusing and poignant as a novice using a multiple-hole pocket sharpener in the manner of a single-blade pocket sharpener — that is, turning a pencil in the starter hole with the expectation of sharpening it entirely. Should you come across such a misguided specimen, loiter a moment in his or her company; you will be rewarded with shrieks of bewilderment as they watch an unsharpened graphite core make its

"Dear God!"

way through the exit hole.

"What's going on?" they will sob, "This sharpener doesn't work! My pencil isn't sharp at all!" Now is the time for intervention, as you place your hand on their shoulder and murmur, *"Friend, you have made a delightful error in judgment. You see, the device you have in hand features two separate holes for different stages of the sharpening process. You have made use of the first hole — and competently, at that, for observe the fine collar shaped by your labors! — but now you must make use of the second. Don't feel ashamed, as yours is a common mistake. The business card I have just slipped in your pocket contains my address, should you feel compelled to reimburse me for the kindness and consultation I have provided."*

Reiterate that, with the graphite core now freed from its cedar casing and exposed to the elements, it is primed for the discipline and focus of the second blade.

STEP THREE: REMOVING THE PENCIL FROM THE FIRST HOLE AND REVIEWING ITS STATUS BEFORE INSERTING IT INTO THE SECOND HOLE

Below is the admittedly unsettling image of our half-finished pencil: The collar has been shaped, but the graphite core remains untouched, having passed through the larger aperture of the first sharpening casement unscathed.

There are some for whom this blunderbuss will be sufficient, offering as it does the maximum diameter of

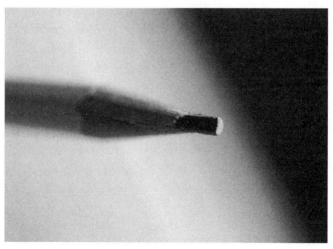

"Wednesday's child" . . . but not for long.

the graphite core.[2] Although there are wider marking surfaces available to pencil points, such surfaces require the pencil be applied at an acute angle to the page. Not so this battering ram: It offers its widest mark when deployed at a perfect right angle, which, in turn, means a minimal risk of breakage, as there is no oblique force acting against it.

Of course, our goal is a sharpened pencil point in the traditional style, which demands tooling this recently exposed graphite rod. Thus are we compelled to put the pencil inside the sharpener's second hole and begin its refinement — provided the length of the exposed core offers a canvas of sufficient size for our masterwork.[3]

STEP FOUR: (SECOND STAGE) SHAPING THE GRAPHITE

Insert the pencil into the second hole in the sharpener, being careful not to chip or damage the intact graphite core. Remember that during this second stage, the sharpener blade will contact graphite exclusively — and therefore requires slightly less torsional force applied to the shaft than necessary when one is shaping wood and graphite simultaneously. (Best to err on the side of not enough force, increasing the "heaviness of hand" as needed.)

---

[2] Here I am thinking of list-makers and/or doodlers suffering from myopia who will appreciate the thick lines and easy legibility of a wide pencil point. I also include sketchers of bears in this group; bear-portraits demand a heavy line so as to capture the burly ferocity of their subjects.

[3] A quarter-inch of exposed graphite should suffice.

This photograph is instructive for two reasons:

1. The short blade of the finishing hole makes it clear that it could not attack a pencil that has not already had its cone shaped, because, at 7/16" (rather than the 7/8" length of a full-sized blade), **it is not long enough to engage a "raw" pencil shaft**. This is obviously a finishing blade, worthless against an unsharpened pencil — a "second hole" if ever there was one.

2. Even though single-blade pocket sharpeners emit a mixture of graphite and cedar when shaping a point, the amount of cedar usually far exceeds the amount of graphite, the latter of which escapes almost unnoticed. In contrast, this "finishing blade" is shaping graphite exclusively, and those users expecting to see more cedar ribbons as per the "starter blade" will be momentarily confused until remembering that, in fact, all the ribbons

of this process have long since unfurled. Such is life: No parade lasts forever. Now we see only graphite exiting the egress slit. However, the byproduct's lack of glamour is more than redeemed by its crucial role in the grander scheme.

(Pursuant to this, users who are new to the multi-hole sharpener and discontented by the site of pure graphite tumbling out of the device unaccompanied by cedar are encouraged to wear a dust mask, if it makes them less anxious.)

Continue shaping the graphite until the pencil turns freely inside the finishing hole. This is your signal to remove the pencil and examine its condition.

How can we be sure the point pictured here was pro-

duced by multi-hole, multi-stage pocket sharpener? The experienced user will note multiple indications.

First, the collar exhibits a ring of indentation where it met the innermost limiting diameter of the second hole.

Second, a close look at the exposed graphite reveals a hint of the unsharpened, cylindrical graphite core at the lower limit of the finishing blade's reach.

Let us also take a moment to commend this point's beautiful collar bottom, one of the finest in this book. The scalloped edges are even at their lowest and highest ends, and run perpendicular to the shaft.[4] Unlike the collar's body, they suggest no hint of the multiple stages involved in this point's creation.[5]

The point itself required no finishing outside the device, as the second stage of sharpening attacked the graphite with single-minded focus and left a tip exhibiting almost no truncation.

Although the multi-hole sharpener requires slightly more work than the single-blade pocket sharpener, I trust some users will find the additional labor rewarding. It produces a collar with numerous intriguing layers that brings to mind a tiered wedding cake, and, as such, makes the perfect nuptial gift.

While a point of this length and sharpness is easily produced by certain hand-crank sharpeners, the diminutive size of the device used here means it is much more easily carried in one's pocket — or, indeed, smuggled unnoticed into forbidding realms. This point, and the humble tool which conjured it, is ideal for those civil servants or flange-turners seeking advanced pencil-pointing in a regulatory environment that disallows the importation of hand-crank mechanisms, or denies a steady surface on which to clamp them.[6]

---

[4] If a scalloped collar bottom is essential to your practice, be wary of some multi-hole sharpeners whose second hole may abrade and flatten the scallops.
[5] And why would they, given that they were formed during the first stage exclusively?
[6] As the reader has no doubt surmised by close review of the attendant technologies, pocket sharpeners can shape shorter pencil stubs than hand-crank sharpeners, further recommending their use by government clerks.

CHAPTER 9:
DECAPITATING A PENCIL POINT: RADICAL TREATMENT IN THE SERVICE OF A GREATER GOOD

IMPORTANT: If the pencil to be decapitated is not your own, make sure to obtain the owner's verbal or written consent before proceeding. Although pencil sharpening offers the full spectrum of human emotion, betrayal, despair and the dark thrill of litigation are best left in the shadows of the unknown.

There is a unique pleasure to be had in renewing the dulled point of a pencil. The obvious analogy is that of polishing a gem so it may more freely shine and exhibit the perfection of its form.[1]

---

[1] I must remember to seek a more obscure and shocking comparison when time permits.

Sadly, as any gemologist knows, there are some stones that languish beyond repair. The same is true of some pencil points. More than once I've had a client present a pencil whose point is so fatally compromised that it cannot be salvaged. In these cases, best practice recommends removing the point from the pencil by force and starting from scratch.

In one of pencil-sharpening's many sobering ironies, we find that eliminating a pencil point requires the same skills as creating one: steady hands; attention to symmetry, smoothness, and other aesthetic ideals; and patience.

We do well to remember that this radical procedure, though it may appear antithetical to sharpening a pencil, is no less a part of our practice than removing an abscessed tooth is to the practice of dentistry. Let us pledge to consider the compromised point with the same respect and dignity we afford the perfected one.

Let us further pledge to destroy it utterly.

Press down on the pencil with your non-dominant hand. The pencil must not wobble under the blade, as this will increase the likelihood of an uneven cut—which would only prolong the suffering.[2]

After confirming the blade is positioned at a right angle to the shaft, **cut into the cedar with consistent pressure**. You may find yourself applying a slight sawing motion — this is acceptable, provided the incision thereby produced is straight.

When you feel the blade contact the graphite core, **stop cutting and turn the pencil**. (If the pencil is hexagonal, rotate it so the neighboring side is now flush with the tabletop; if the pencil is cylindrical, rotate it 60 degrees.) Cut into the pencil again, making sure the new incision is perpendicular to the shaft and aligned with the previous cut.

---

[2] If the pencil wobbles, remember: This phenomenon is likely caused by an uneven cutting surface or an irregular shaft; it is not the terrified death-shudder of the pencil itself. As much as we invest our cedar friends with fond affection, they are inanimate objects, and, as such, incapable of feeling pain or despair. (All the more reason to envy them!)

Continue cutting and rotating until you've produced a single, unbroken incision around the shaft.

Now the only thing keeping your pencil in one piece is its graphite core. It is time to sever this bond. With a final, forceful application of the blade, **cut through the graphite**. The point should fall clean away from the shaft.

The deed is done.

Cutting into the shaft of a pencil and removing its point can be an emotionally wrenching experience. After all, as pencil sharpeners we are taught to perfect and protect the point at all costs, and this amputation may feel perverse and unjust.

If the process leaves you feeling bereft or ashamed (see photo, overleaf), **take a moment to wipe your brow** and regain your composure while recalling this verse from Elinor Wylie's "Address to My Soul":

The pure integral form,
Austere and silver-dark,
Is balanced on the storm
In its predestined arc.[3]

---

[3] If there is any doubt this 1928 poem is about the fragility of pencil points ("austere and silver-dark"), and seeks to comfort the agitated pencil sharpener who finds him- or herself "balanced on the storm" of pencil decapitation, we need only remember the second verse and its obvious reference to the durability of plastic display tubes:

Fear not, pathetic flame;
Your sustenance is doubt:
Glassed in translucent dream
They cannot snuff you out.

You have nothing to be ashamed of.

Rest assured your melancholy will be displaced by satisfaction soon enough, as the "predestined arc" of the pencil point is conjured anew by your hand.

To ensure the best possible conditions for making a new point, even out any irregularities in the freshly exposed pencil top by sanding it down.

What was once a compromised pencil should now look as unblemished and full of promise as any fresh from the box!

You are now free to make a new point.

ANTIQUE PENCIL SHARPENERS: A REVERIE

Like drugs, pencil sharpening techniques have their gateways of delight. Readers who are intimidated by using a pocketknife may ease into the practice via a pivot-blade Little Shaver sharpener. The one pictured here was manufactured in the early 1900s; a modern replica is available from Lee Valley Tools.

The Little Shaver employs a straight blade moving parallel to the pencil shaft like a pocketknife. The pivoting arm limits erratic motion and offers a fine introduction to the art of moderating blade pressure and cutting-depth.

Once you have savored the pleasures of the gateway, you may proceed to the mansions beyond!

CHAPTER 10:
USING A DOUBLE-BURR
HAND-CRANK SHARPENER

EQUIPMENT CHECKLIST:
- Double-burr hand-crank pencil sharpener
- Pencil

ONCE YOU FEEL COMFORTABLE USING A single-burr hand-crank sharpener, it may be appropriate to advance to the double-burr example of this technology. The operating principle of the double-burr sharpener is simply an escalation of that of the single-burr: Namely, two cylinder blades now rotate around the pencil to shape its point.

Double-burr sharpening mechanism

The pencil sharpener used in this chapter is an extraordinary example of engineering: The El Casco M430-CN. Based in the Basque region of Spain, the El Casco[1] company began as a manufacturer of handguns; the economic climate of the Great Depression required a diversification of product, and the family-run business began producing high-end office equipment. (One thinks fondly of Isaiah 2:4.) Per the company web site, "all precision components are individually numbered and assembled by hand."

While this device is by no means typical of double-burr hand-crank sharpeners — far more common are the wall-mounted sharpeners found in classrooms — I trust your author will be forgiven for celebrating it in this

[1] In English, "The Helmet."

chapter. Rest assured the principles behind its use are fundamentally the same as those for any double-burr hand-crank sharpener.

Should you include an El Casco in your arsenal? It depends on the budget you have allotted for your practice. As to its cost, I will only say the El Casco pictured here is the fourth-most expensive thing I own — and I own a house and a car.

STEP ONE: STABILIZING THE SHARPENER

As discussed in Chapter 7, every hand-crank sharpener — whether single- or double-burr — must be stabilized while in use. The El Casco is no different, but forgoes the traditional table-clamp in favor of a handsome rubber suction base.

To stabilize the sharpener, **turn the lever to create a vacuum** between the table top and the base of the machine.

Some readers may be unsettled by the sequence of events recorded above, and protest: "Why are we now told to stabilize the sharpener *before* inserting the pencil? When using the single-burr hand-crank sharpener, we were told to stabilize the sharpener *after* inserting the pencil!"

This apparent inconsistency is due to the fact that in our single-burr paradigm, we stabilized the device with our hand, rather than with a table clamp — inserting the pencil *after* stabilizing the sharpener would require the user to do with one hand what is typically done with two (as one hand is needed to extend the spring-loaded intake mechanism).

STEP TWO: "DIAL M FOR MURDER"

The El Casco offers four different settings for graphite exposure and point length; **adjusting a dial on the end of the handle moves a spring-loaded point limiter into position**.

As my clients are aficionados of extreme pencil-pointing, they usually insist on maximum graphite exposure.

STEP THREE: "WE PROMISE TO VISIT EVERY WEEK, GRANDMOTHER": INTRODUCING THE PENCIL TO ITS NEW HOME

Like many of our single-burr hand-crank friends, this device has an iris-like aperture for centering the pencil within the sharpening mechanism. Opening its "eye" is a simple matter of moving a lever atop the aperture casing.

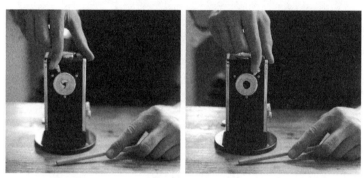

"Dream your dreams with open eyes." —T. E. Lawrence

Insert the pencil through the sharpener's iris and into its body.[2]

STEP FOUR: ROTATING THE CRANK HANDLE

Holding the pencil parallel to the surface on which the sharpener rests, **begin rotating the crank handle**. (The crank-handle process is similar to that of the single-burr hand-crank sharpener; see Chapter 7.)

As this sharpener does not have a spring-loaded

---

[2] Please keep in mind that in this case, "sharpener" refers to the machine, not its user.

intake mechanism, you alone are responsible for moving the pencil into the rotating burrs. **Do so now**.

STEP FIVE: "ENJOYING THE VIEW"

The El Casco, unlike most hand-crank sharpeners, has an observation window for monitoring the rotational orbit of the burrs. If you are using the device in public, rest assured the window's glass will soon be fogged by the breath of curious onlookers.

This observation window is not just a gimmick; it also functions as a clever pedagogical device, a "skylight" through which the rays of understanding illuminate an oft-obscure technology. You should exploit "peeping Toms'" curiosity by enlightening them as to the mechanics of burr cylinders and their sharpening methods.

Do not allow onlookers to touch the pencil sharpener.

STEP SIX: HALTING THE OPERATION
SO AS TO INSPECT THE PENCIL POINT

As the burrs find less resistance and the crank
handle's rotations become smoother, **taper your crank-
rate** before bringing the process to a halt. (If you have set
the device for maximum graphite exposure, you should
expect to make between 65 and 80 rotations before stop-
ping.)

Open the aperture, remove the pencil, and inspect the
point. If it is satisfactory, record the number of handle-
rotations in your log. If it is not, **carefully reinsert the
pencil and continue the sharpening process.**[3]

---

[3] Be mindful of the risk of breaking the pencil's point when reinserting it into
the sharpener (see Chapter 12).

STEP SEVEN: FORMING A MORE PERFECT TIP

The El Casco's documentation includes this caveat: *"The sharpening mechanism is designed to put a slightly different point on the pencil than you are used to seeing. The tip of the point is slightly flat, which avoids the problem of the point breaking when you first touch the paper."*

If you wish to put a finer tip on the pencil, the device features a serrated lip on its shavings drawer, angled so that graphite swarf falls inside.[4]

---

[4] The use of metal files to finish pencil points has a long tradition. (See page 117.)

Let us examine a pencil point typical of the El Casco, if not the average double-burr sharpener. The observant reader will note two important differences between this point and the one shaped by the single-burr sharpener in Chapter 7: the scalloped edges where the shaft gives way to the exposed-cedar collar are less pronounced than those produced by the single-burr machine; and the collar is actually concave, with a slight curve to its profile.[5]

It is also significant that, though both machines were set for maximum graphite exposure and produced collars of equal height, the (double-burr) El Casco's point boasts at least 30% more graphite than that of the (single-burr) Dahle 166. Finishing the former's point on the shavings

---

[5] The unusual shape of the collar is due to the bifurcated shaping sleeve inside the sharpening mechanism, which is slightly convex. As the shaft of the pencil moves into the sleeve, it is molded like clay on a potter's wheel.

drawer has further refined its elegance.[6]

This is a stylish pencil point indeed, manifesting a peculiar sophistication that seems so resolutely European we can scarcely believe it was conjured in an American workshop. When presented with such a point, the natural inclination for many pencil enthusiasts will be to treat it as an *objet d'art*; they would no more think of applying this point to the page than they would think of eating a Fabergé egg or going pee-pee in Marcel Duchamp's famous art-toilet. This natural inclination (could it be intimidation?) is forgivable — but the client is also encouraged to discover those pleasures available when the pencil is put to use.

And who would use such a pencil point? Given their cost and exclusivity, there is little doubt that most El Cascos will be found idling on the desks of CEOs, as they are actively marketed as executive gifts.[7] How often and with what appreciation these titans of industry actually use their El Cascos is unknown; it is not inconceivable that the concept of "placing pearls before swine" may be applicable in some cases.

But there are other professionals whose needs could be met by such a point, as its length offers maximum visibility of the line regardless of the pencil's position relative to the page and the user's position relative to the pencil.

---

[6] Of course, we must make note of the slight imperfection in the graphite approximately ⅛ of the way down the point. This is the result of uneven finishing, and serves to illustrate the importance of rotating the point slowly and evenly while running it against an abrasive finishing surface.

[7] The El Casco pictured in this chapter is also available in 23-carat gold.

There is little doubt industrial engineers would favor this point for drafting schematic diagrams — and they would certainly appreciate the marvelous device which produced it.[8] Similarly, artists who sketch insect wings, apple seeds, and other small objects will appreciate the fine line and focus of the El Casco's output.

A NOTE ABOUT SHAVINGS

Of all the sharpeners in my tool kit, the El Casco produces the most finely ground shavings. Many single- and double-burr sharpeners' swarf presents as pleasing curlicues; not so the El Casco's — its burrs so pulverize the cedar and graphite that they look like ash. During live events I always warn clients that, should they choose the El Casco, they will be rewarded with an extraordinary point, but their bag of shavings will look biohazardous.

Clients sometimes ask for suggestions as to what to do with their pencil shavings. I believe no use approaches the simplicity and beauty of displaying the shavings alongside the pencil; the traditional uses listed below are included only in the interest of comprehensiveness.

---

[8] Some will object that engineers rarely use #2 pencils, preferring instead the finer line and harder tip of the #4 or 9H. The objection is not without merit — I mean only to suggest that, should an engineer find him- or herself stranded on an island with nothing but a box of #2 pencils, an array of sharpeners, and an incorrigible desire to design a life raft, his or her needs would best be served by a double-burr device like the El Casco. If the island's inventory does not include an El Casco, our castaway should forage for a CARL Angel-5 or other single-burr sharpener that produces a notably long point.

10.1: USES FOR SINGLE-BLADE POCKET SHARPENER
RIBBON-STYLE SHAVINGS (COARSE)

Kindling

Mulch

Props for still-life paintings of pencil shavings

Fingertip cedar-scenters (rub shavings between thumb and fingers to release fragrance)

Closet moth repellant (this will require multiple pencils' shavings, unless the closet is very small)

False moustache/soul patch ("jazz disguise")

Disposable drink coaster (assemble the shavings in a tight grouping before placing a glass on them)

Sugar-free gum substitute

Nicotine-free chewing tobacco substitute

Food-free snack substitute

Facial-oil blotters

Imitation scabs (ideal for blindfolded haunted-house games)

10.2: USES FOR SINGLE-BURR HAND-CRANK SHARPENER
CURLICUE-STYLE SHAVINGS (MEDIUM)

Compost

Stuffing for doll pillows

Cupcake-icing texturizer (not recommended)

Cat litter (will require multiple pencils' worth of shavings, unless the cat's bowel movements are extremely small)

Novelty gift: "Pinocchio's sneeze collection"

Easter basket filling

Mouse-coffin filling

Pile

10.3: USES FOR DOUBLE-BURR HAND-CRANK
SHARPENER DUST-STYLE SHAVINGS (FINE)

Low-cost eye shadow replacement (not recommended)

Ashtray fill

Prop drugs (ideal for high-school plays about drugs)

Coal substitute for extraction-mining dioramas

Fingertip de-cleansers (rub shavings between thumb and fingers)

Ninja-style blinding dust (blow directly into the eyes of attacker)

Squirrel tracker (dip squirrel's feet in bowl of shavings; track squirrel's movements by following trail of graphite/cedar residue)

Baby tracker (see above)

"Emo dust"

ANTIQUE PENCIL SHARPENERS: A REVERIE

Perhaps the most elegant example of using a file to finish a pencil point, the 19th century Perfect Pencil Pointer required the user to expose a pencil's lead with a knife before placing it in the circular handle and rotating it along a metal file. These devices now command up to $2,500 (depending on condition) and are not necessary items in the novice's tool kit.

CHAPTER 11:
A FEW WORDS ABOUT
MECHANICAL PENCILS

Mechanical pencils are bullshit.

CHAPTER 12:
PSYCHOLOGICAL RISKS ASSOCIATED WITH PENCIL SHARPENING: ASSESSMENT AND COPING STRATEGIES

EVERY ASPECT OF PENCIL SHARPENING includes its own suite of pleasures and anxieties. The pleasures should be familiar to you; we turn now to the anxieties.

Although sharpening a pencil is usually a psychologically rewarding experience, resulting in feelings of accomplishment and serenity, it also entails psychological risks. It is your professional and personal responsibility to be aware of these risks, and to actively discourage their flourishing in your practice.

DISAPPOINTING THE CLIENT

The greatest anxiety, at least for me, is disappointing my clients. Whether you're sharpening a pencil in front of a crowd or alone in your workshop for a distant stranger, the weight of expectation can disturb an otherwise balanced mind.

It is during these paid "gigs" that your relationship to your pencil sharpeners is most like that of a musician to his or her instrument. It is incumbent on the performer to ensure his or her instrument is operating at maximum capacity. This means, of course, tending for it; tuning it; maintaining and optimizing its functionality; and treating it with the respect it deserves—while ensuring others do as well.

The more care you invest in your pencil sharpening tools, the more familiar you are with their strengths and their idiosyncrasies, the more confident you can be during their use. This will in turn reduce your anxiety—freeing up space in your consciousness for more profitable thoughts.

Keep your blades sharp. Keep your burr cylinders clean. Keep your eyes on the task at hand. This will go a long away towards keeping your demons at bay.

ANXIETY OF THE UNKNOWN: THE UNSHARPENED PENCIL

Even if you are confident about your practice, familiar with your tools, and certain of your ability to make the best use of them, there is yet another element of the pencil-sharpening experience to consider. It is the one clients pay the most attention to, with good reason—for this element is the sharpener's *raison d'etre*: the pencil.

Ironically, the client's pencil is simultaneously the most crucial element of the job and the element you will be least familiar with—for (unless you're renewing a point you've previously sharpened) you will be approaching it for the first time. This is why it's crucial to have confidence in your ability to size up any pencil the client offers, or confidence in any pencil you yourself provide.

As we've discussed before, an easy way to reduce anxiety and improve the chance of sharpening success is to **make sure the pencil's shaft is straight**, the **graphite is centered within the wood**, and the **unsharpened top is free of paint** (see Chapter 2). It's also worth reminding the client that a poorly manufactured pencil can only play host to a point of mediocre quality; we cannot expect a five-star meal from a one-star restaurant. Saying this in a loud voice will comfort the client — they will know they are in good hands. Your confidence will be bolstered in turn.

PERFORMANCE ANXIETY: THE LIVE PENCIL-SHARPENING EXPERIENCE

Any professional pencil sharpener worth his or her salt will have road stories about hecklers and unforgiving customers who seem incapable of accepting that every pencil is different, and some will carry scooped collars or other irregularities to their grave. We must not be discouraged by obnoxious reactions to our craft; instead, **record any wounding taunts or sarcastic remarks in your log** along with a physical description of their authors. Then commission a comedian or bartender to compose witty responses and mail them to the offending party.

EMOTIONAL RISKS ASSOCIATED WITH DIFFERENT PENCIL-POINTING TECHNIQUES

As the reader now knows, each method of sharpening a pencil produces a different point — a result of its unique technology and operation. Is it any wonder, then, that each method is also attended by its unique forebodings and disquietudes?

Below is a partial list of the emotional risks associated with particular sharpening techniques.[1]

Single-Blade Pocket Sharpener:

Any discussion of the psychological risks associated with single-blade pocket sharpeners must begin with the tyranny of the irregular pin tip. The agony of removing a pencil from the device, only to find an errant filigree of graphite branching away from the point's end, will be a familiar sensation to the novice — and is hardly unknown to the professional.

Fortunately, an irregular pin tip is less a verdict of one's failures as a craftsman and human being as it is an argument for further diligence and research. One of the many psychological benefits of maintaining a pencil-sharpening log is the comfort of actionable data it provides. If you find yourself producing irregular pin tips with unseemly regularity, simply **review your log** for the average number of rotations and applications of force you apply with a single-blade pocket sharpener, and adjust accordingly.

A second psychological risk associated with single-blade pocket sharpeners is the terror that they will be misplaced and lost due to their diminutive size. I myself used to suffer from this distraction until, recalling the age-old advice of finding "a place for everything, and everything in its place," I constructed a pocket-sharpener compartment system for my tool kit, and pledged to return any

---

[1] Specific antique sharpeners may also provide succor. (See page 155.)

pocket sharpener to its tiny cubicle as soon as its job was finished. An afternoon's work served to eliminate a year's worth of worry. Such is the nature of investing in one's well-being — the dividends are exponential, if not infinite.

Hand-Crank Sharpeners (Single- And Double-Burr):

The reader may insist that hand-crank sharpeners, being the most consistent and predictable of our pencil-pointing devices, are incapable of causing psychological distress. As counterargument I offer two difficult situations the hand-crank user may encounter:

1. Removing a pencil from a hand-crank sharpener for inspection, only to find that the graphite point has broken off inside the device, leaving you with a "hollow collar" — a finished collar with a hole where the graphite should be.[2] (See Chapter 2.) The unhappy absence where one was expecting abundance may well trigger unwanted associations with financial, intellectual, and romantic aspects of your own life. **Ignore them**. Amputate the empty collar, clear the sharpener's burrs of the forfeit point, and set course for the future abundances that are your due.

2. Inspecting a hand-cranked point, determining it isn't sharp enough, and then reinserting it into the sharpener, only to break the point upon its reinsertion — thereby destroying your investment of sweat equity by your own hand. This phenomenon, perhaps the most frustrating

---

[2] Also known as a "headless horseman" or a "Louis XVI," a hollow collar is most often caused by internal breakage of the pencil's graphite core somewhere below the collar top. Unless you make a habit of throwing pencils against the wall before sharpening them, it is not your fault. Few things are.

in the trade, is known as the "Malleus Maleficarum," because, like the 15th century witch-hunting text for which it is named, it suggests the existence of satanic conspiracy.[3] Again, consider this unholy accident an opportunity for recalibration of your technique: The next time you reinsert a semi-sharpened pencil into a hand-crank sharpener, **do so with greater delicacy** so as to minimize the chance of breaking the point against the static burrs. I have little doubt your odds of catastrophe will diminish.

Knife:

Of all pencil-pointing technologies, surely the knife promises the deepest wellspring of potential emotional hazards, as its threat is simultaneously literal, archetypal, and Freudian. (Those suffering from aichmophobia[4] are reminded that there is no shame in omitting knives from their practice.)

---

[3] Although the *Malleus Maleficarum* pre-dates the modern pencil by almost 100 years, a sufficiently metaphorical reading of the following passage suggests the Devil's hand is indeed to blame when pencil points are removed by hand-crank sharpeners:

"Here is declared the truth about diabolic operations with regard to the male organ. And to make plain the facts in this matter, it is asked whether witches can with the help of devils really and actually remove the member, or whether they only do so apparently by some glamour or illusion. And that they can actually do so is argued a fortiori; for since devils can do greater things than this ... therefore they can also truly and actually remove men's members."

[4] Per Wikipedia, aichmophobia is "the morbid fear of sharp things, such as *pencils*, needles, knives, a pointing finger, or even the sharp end of an umbrella ..." (Emphasis added, to argue that the ranks of top-seeded pencil-sharpening aichmophobes may be thin indeed.)

The pocketknife in your tool kit may host an additional profusion of anxieties, if, like mine, it belonged to your late grandfather — a successful research chemist, amateur astronomer, and woodworker who lived through the Great Depression, built his own telescope, voted Republican, and kept his hair in a neat buzz cut. You may find it difficult to use the tool for your pencil-sharpening business without feeling a clammy apprehension that somewhere, a ghost is rolling his eyes at you. No matter: Though ours may not be the "Greatest Generation," we can still insist on fumbling towards greatness on our own terms.

THE IMPORTANCE OF MAINTAINING A HEALTHY ATTITUDE TOWARDS ONE'S PRACTICE IN THE FACE OF BROKEN PENCIL POINTS, PHYSICAL EXHAUSTION, SOCIETAL DISAPPROVAL, SEXUAL IMPOTENCE, AND FINANCIAL RUIN

In the end, even the most accomplished pencil sharpener must concede that absolute perfection, while an appropriate goal, is rarely attained. Pencil sharpening takes place in the unforgiving glare of the physical world, and is subject to the same contingencies and calamities that bedevil all things material.[5] Happily, however, like any

[5] For instance, as I finish this chapter late at night, my sedan's car alarm keeps going off—to the delight of my neighbors, no doubt. (One of whom is a bald, burly mechanic and one of whom is a tattoo-covered prison guard [female], both of whom could probably break a bundle of pencils with their bare hands.) However, as automobiles are material objects, we must learn to live with their shortcomings, as I will remind my neighbors in the morning before being beaten to death.

earthly specimen, our practice (whether "sweet, sour; adazzle, dim") may thus lay claim to those glories of "pied beauty" celebrated by Gerard Manley Hopkins.[6]

We must learn to live with — perhaps even savor — the uncertainties and imperfections that attend every pencil point, even as we continue to strive for their ideal form. This is not an admission of futility so much as a considered reflection on the vagaries of human experience and the importance of appreciating one's circumstance even as one seeks to improve it.

It is in this spirit that I invite the reader to heed the following words, not in my capacity as a pencil sharpener, but as a friend:

The only perfection available to you without compromise is that of intention and effort. If you endeavor to be the best pencil sharpener you can be, and tailor your actions accordingly, you can be certain all else will be forgiven in the final accounting.

With these words I have solved all psychological problems.

---

[6] Glory be to God for dappled things —
For skies of couple-colour as a brinded cow;
For rose-moles all in stipple upon trout that swim;
Fresh-firecoal chestnut-falls; finches' wings;
Landscape plotted and pieced — fold, fallow, and plough;
And áll trádes, their gear and tackle and trim.

All things counter, original, spare, strange;
Whatever is fickle, freckled (who knows how?)
With swift, slow; sweet, sour; adazzle, dim;
He fathers-forth whose beauty is past change:
Praise him.

ONE NIGHT ONLY
SATURDAY AT THE ARENA:
THRLL to the CONTEST of
MAN vs. MACHINE!

DAVID REES ★★★★ *PANASONIC KP-310*
★ ARTISANAL PENCILSMITH ★   ★ ELECTRONIC AUTO-STOP ★
"OL' STEADY HAND"   "IT NEVER SLEEPS"
THE ONLY STEEL...IS IN HIS NERVE   *NO PENCIL IS SAFE FROM ITS JAWS*

WHO WILL BE APPOINTED KING?
~ SAFETY GOGGLES A MUST!! ~

CHAPTER 13:
HOW TO USE AN
ELECTRIC PENCIL SHARPENER

EQUIPMENT CHECKLIST:
- Electric pencil sharpener
- Mallet
- Safety goggles

YOU WOULDN'T TRUST AN ELECTRIC MACHINE
to deliver your baby; why would you trust one to sharpen
your pencil? And yet millions of desks are darkened by
electric pencil sharpeners — a testament to the office-
supply industry's hordes of mind-manipulators.

We are all familiar with the relentless, miserly whine
of the electric sharpener. We recognize the artless pencil

point that is its eschatology.[1] We argue against their use to friends and family — and still they fly off the shelves. Why?

A clue can be found on the web site of Hammacher Schlemmer — famous purveyors of gizmos and absurdities for the aspirational American[2] — where the store's "History" page boasts of selling the world's first electric pencil sharpener. Apparently people still believe this device is the ultimate status symbol; a way to announce that one has "arrived"; an object whose possession magically confers upon its owner the status of intelligentsia, renegade, elite.

Yet the sad fact is that almost every supposed advantage of the electric pencil sharpener has been exaggerated beyond recognition.

To take but one example: The vaunted "efficiency" of electric pencil sharpeners is overrated: They are worthless on a camping trip; a blackout instantly changes them into paperweights; they can hardly be counted on to work in a waterfall.[3] "Oh," the electric pencil sharpener enthusiast may object, "but my electric pencil sharpener

---

[1] Is it hyperbole to suggest that guiding a cedar pencil into the maw of the electric pencil sharpener is a degradation — the equivalent of coitus with an inflatable doll? The act may be a sexual one, but it's not lovemaking. It is, instead, a simulacram of intimacy. And insofar as it represents the null set of seduction, it is dehumanizing.

[2] From the store's Wikipedia entry: "In the 1960s, Hammacher Schlemmer offered products that had never been available for home purchase, including a regulation-sized bowling alley and restored London taxi cabs." The man who buys a bowling alley out of a box is a man to be slapped on the back of the head with great enthusiasm.

[3] See Chapter 16.

is different — it runs on batteries!" Has our protesting Pollyanna given any thought to what a useless folly his amazing battery-operated pencil sharpener will be the moment our world runs out of batteries? Likely not.

To my mind, the greatest shortcoming of the electric pencil sharpener is not its limited utility, but the way it alienates its user from the pencil-sharpening process. In a culture that prizes openness and accountability, this device remains a defiantly closed system; the ultimate black box; a windowless abattoir.[4]

Nevertheless, electric pencil sharpeners must be counted among pencil-pointing technologies, and therefore fall under this book's purview. I can only endeavor to show you the most effective means of using these devices, and hope you do so as often as possible.

STEP ONE: PAYING ATTENTION

If your pencil-sharpening practice finds you strolling the avenues and byways of your town, sharpening kit in hand, **pay attention to your surroundings**. You never know when you may come across a property whose occupants are electric pencil sharpener users, and passing by without comment or intervention would be a crime. (To be sure, our craft confers all the pleasures and responsibilities of the deputized.)

---

[4] It's disheartening to note how many "computer nerds" — who so often complain about closed proprietary software and condemn restrictive end-user license agreements — are perfectly content to entrust their pencils to a device whose mechanics and engineering resist inspection and refinement.

If it's a sunny day, you should wear a wide-brimmed hat for UV protection. Choose a stylish one.

It's no wonder this house has stopped me in my tracks. Let us review the signs that suggest a certain appliance therein:

1. **Pencil markings** on porch steps indicate the presence of pencils;
2. **Air conditioning unit** indicates the presence of electricity;
3. **Closely mowed lawn** indicates a preoccupation with orderliness, and yet;
4. **Disorderly porch** indicates limited free time;
5. **Banality of architecture** indicates disinterest in aesthetics and craftsmanship.

Our quarry at rest (see lower left corner of photograph)

All signs point toward the presence of an electrical pencil sharpener inside.

STEP TWO: ENTERING THE WORK AREA

As we are not blessed with X-ray vision, and as the government doesn't maintain public records of pencil sharpener ownership, and as confronting the occupants could be awkward, and as the occupants seem to be out of the house anyway, the only way to confirm your suspicions is to **enter the home and look around**.

First-floor windows with flimsy screens are ideal entry-points. If it's winter, your passage may be complicated by storm windows. In this situation, it's advisable to **make note of the property's address** and return when warmer weather arrives.

It is important to bring your entire body inside the house, as neighbors' suspicions may be aroused if they notice something hanging out the window.

STEP THREE: SEARCHING THE RESIDENCE FOR OFFENDING DEVICES

Once you're completely inside the property, confirm your hunch and justify your ingress by scanning the residence for electric pencil sharpeners, keeping in mind that they may be below or behind you.

If you don't find an electric pencil sharpener after an hour or so, courtesy demands you leave.

Fortunately, in this situation I needn't feel uncomfortable about entering a stranger's home, as there is an electric pencil sharpener in plain view. Closer inspection reveals it to be a Boston sharpener (Model 18) from the late 20th Century. Why is it here? Perhaps its owner is a Massachusetts native and keeps it for nostalgic effect. Perhaps it is simply admired as an example of the "beige brick" school of industrial design. A third possibility is

that the owner has simply forgotten it entirely, and no longer registers its unfortunate presence in his or her work area.

There is also the depressing chance that the owner actively uses it to sharpen pencils.

Regardless of the reason, this unhappy home is infested. But its hour of liberation is at hand.

It is time to make use of the device.

STEP FOUR: DISARMING THE SHARPENER

The first step in using an electric pencil sharpener is to unplug it. **Trace the electrical cord** from the back of the sharpener to the wall outlet, taking care not to inadvertently skip over to another item's cord. If your eyes can't be trusted, use your hand: You don't want to risk unplugging the wrong electrical device, as this could

complicate your unknown hosts' forthcoming gratitude.

With a firm, steady grip, **unplug the pencil sharpener from the outlet**.

The sharpener has been disarmed.

STEP FIVE: CHOOSING THE BEST TOOL FOR THE JOB

Remove the sharpener from the desk and place it in the middle of the largest room in the house. Again, this logic is dictated by etiquette: You don't want to damage furnishings during use.

The choice of tool for effective use of the pencil sharpener should be an easy one. As you can see in this photograph, I had the appropriate items on hand; if your kit does not include a mallet or hammer, feel free to scour the residence. (Remember to return any tools when your job is done![5])

Now is the time for a final inspection of the pencil sharpener. In addition to analyzing the casing for cracks,

---

[5] It may help to tie a long string from the handle of the tool to the place from where it was taken, as a reminder of its proper location. A trail of pencil shavings also works in a pinch.

weathering, or other pre-existent weaknesses that may smooth your operation, you should **take note of any manufacturer's information** that could lend an air of poignancy or poetic justice to the proceedings.

According to the manufacturer's label on the bottom, the Boston Model 18 pictured here was assembled in Statesville, NC — and it shall meet its destiny at the hands of a North Carolinian. We could not ask for a more fortuitous turn of events.

STEP SIX: GETTING TO WORK

Tighten your safety goggles, raise the mallet over your head, and **bring it down on the body of the electric sharpener** with maximum force. Repeat as necessary.

When the mallet-head connects with the sharpener your impulse may be to blink or duck your head. Remember that you have nothing to fear — goggles are protecting your eyes — and endeavor to maintain visual contact with the sharpener, as a piece of it may break off and come hurtling at you.

Some people prefer to use electric sharpeners while sitting on the floor with legs apart. In addition to greater stability, this position allows you to contain flying debris with your thighs.

Continue making use of the sharpener. You should work in silence. The impulse to howl in ecstasy; deliver a full-throated monologue about the dignity of hand-labor and the decadence of mechanization; or simply scream "DIE! DIE! MY DARLING!" should be resisted, however tempting. Such outbursts will only draw attention from passersby, and encourage invasive queries from busybody neighbors.

If you feel your energy flagging, and the home's decorations indicate especially permissive and forgiving occupants (see Table 13.1), it may be appropriate to forage in their refrigerator.

13.1: ITEMS IN THE HOME WHICH MAY INDICATE ESPECIALLY PERMISSIVE AND FORGIVING OCCUPANTS

Windows
Welcome mats
Wind chimes
Crystals
Books
Unopened bills on kitchen counter
"DO BONGS" spray-painted on garage door
"North American Marijuana-Smoking Champion" trophy covered in Mardi Gras beads
Colorful objects
Wooden die-cut plaques that say "Bless This Mess"
Wooden die-cut plaques that say "I Don't Give A Shit About Anything"
Dust bunnies
Framed photographs of vegetables
Old typewriters
An orgy
Nutritional yeast flakes

Children's crayon marks on the wall
Sitar where the television should be
Unsorted cutlery in silverware drawer
Unsorted underwear in underwear drawer
Bar soap
Throw pillows
Foreign coins mixed in with regular coins in coin jar
Montessori-school pamphlets
"Native" rugs
Scented candles
Candles
Matches
No fire extinguisher
Stray LEGOS (see photograph)
Stray copies of the Oberlin Alumni Magazine
Feral dogs
Plants
An electric pencil sharpener

Once the sharpener's housing has been smashed, you can trade your mallet for a smaller hammer (or hammers, as I have done here) to focus on detailed atomization of the device.

Using an electric pencil sharpener is unlike using a manual pencil sharpener in that there is no pencil involved. Because of this, there is no obvious terminus to the job, as you cannot refer to the progress of the pencil point as a guide. You should use your own judgment in deciding when to stop using an electric pencil sharpener. If you look at the scattered remains and catch yourself murmuring, *"No way will that busted-ass piece of shit ever sharpen a pencil again,"* it's a good indication that you have satisfied the Platonic ideal of its utility.

STEP SEVEN: BAGGING THE SHARPENER

When I was a Cub Scout, I was taught to observe the rule: "Leave your camp site cleaner than you found it." It behooves us to follow the spirit of these words in our use of electric pencil sharpeners, although leaving something cleaner than you found it is a logical and logistical impossibility, and, as such, may be ignored.

This is not to say we shouldn't tidy up after ourselves. Decency requires us to collect and bag the electric sharpener — in addition to honoring the principles of fastidiousness and organization that animate our practice, it will go a long way toward convincing the homeowners that artisanal pencil sharpeners are a thoughtful breed.

Using your tweezers, **collect the used sharpener and place its remains in a large transparent bag**. If your utilization was a dynamic affair, with pieces flying about the room, you should take extra care to gather them all.

If you're not sure if you've gathered all the pieces, try this simple test: Hold the debris-filled bag. Does it feel as heavy as the electric pencil sharpener did before you used it? If it does, you can be sure you've collected all the pieces. If the bag feels lighter than the intact sharpener did, there are pieces yet to gather. **Gather them**.

When the last piece has been deposited into the bag, seal it shut. **Return the bagged sharpener to its original location**.

I usually leave an explanatory note with the bagged remains for the benefit my unknown friends. I include my name and address in case they would enjoy further correspondence.[6]

STEP EIGHT: GETTING THE FUCK OUT

When your work is done you should return any tools, personal effects, or drug paraphernalia to their original locations. If you made use of the household's kitchen, wash and dry your dishes.

It is now time to vacate the property.

If your exit is observed by neighborhood children, you may be able to buy their discretion by offering them a complimentary pencil sharpening (see Chapter 14).

---

[6] Although a gratuity is appropriate, I have found that modern homeowners rarely observe this protocol. Perhaps they're too busy slouching towards Gomorrah to remember the decencies and kindnesses that bind our culture together — or perhaps they regularly misplace my name and address. Regardless, in my experience a follow-up courtesy call soliciting remuneration is rarely worth the effort.

Leaving through the same window you entered means you won't have to damage a second one.

Dear David,

I was SO So So **FLABBER-GAASTED** when I saw the pencils. When Miriam said "we have a surprise" I thought the "surprise" was we all are going to get a **wand** (special wand). But when she took the pencils out they looked perfect and great.

SO THANK you FOR the :

(P.S Why are the pencils so expensiv)

CHAPTER 14

SHARPENING PENCILS FOR CHILDREN

EQUIPMENT CHECKLIST:

- Animal-themed pocket
  sharpener
- Candy

- Two pencils
- Children
  (not pictured)

CHILDREN ARE FASCINATED BY PENCILS,
even if they don't understand them. Opening the doors
of your practice to young people allows you to de-mystify
the work of a pencil sharpener. It also teaches children to
value integrity, craftsmanship, and capitalist ingenuity.

Parents or teachers planning their next birthday
party or school field trip would do well to remember the

artisanal pencil sharpener. A rewarding time can be had by all, provided the children are not unruly and bring their own sandwiches.

STEP ONE: CHILD-PROOFING YOUR WORKPLACE

From the moment they cross the threshold of your workplace until the moment they leave, children's safety is your responsibility. Before their arrival, take a few minutes to make sure your workplace is child-appropriate: Clear the area of **pocket knives**, **box cutters**, **stray piles of pencil shavings**, **alcohol** and other **industrial lubricants**, and **any pencil sharpener worth more than two dollars**.

If parents register concern about their kids visiting a professional pencil sharpener, you can put them at ease with a curt reminder that a pencil's "lead" doesn't contain actual lead. Their children may eat pencil shavings all day without fear of lead poisoning.

If their children attend an expensive New England private school, a casual mention of Henry David Thoreau's career as a pencil manufacturer should lend the visit a patina of Yankee exclusivity that most parents will find irresistible.

If their children attend an under-funded public school, a casual mention of free pencils should suffice.[1]

---

[1] If their children are home-schooled, an extended monologue about the Federal Reserve, the Zionist evolution conspiracy, and/or the vaccination mafia will likely result in a dinner invitation.

14.1: COMMON NAMES OF AMERICAN SCHOOLCHILDREN

Bobby	Margie	Tori
Sammy	Mindy	Lori
Sally	Frankie	Laurie
Tommy	Johnny	Barry
Timmy	Dougie	Larry
Jimmy	Ellie	Carrie
Jenny	Kelly	Gary
Willy	Mickey	Harry
Wally	Mikey	Perry
Charlie	Millie	Percy
Chuckie	Minnie	Darcy
Mary	Louie	Ernie
Jenny	Jamie	Bernie
Betty	Gordy	Barney
Freddy	Davey	Robby
Ollie	Abby	Blobby
Holly	Annie	Billy
Nelly	Jerry	Jeffy
Polly	Terry	Dolly
Maggie	Terri	PJ

14.2: UNCOMMON NAMES OF AMERICAN SCHOOLCHILDREN

Ziffy	Beigey	Truckie
Stumpy	Snakey	Paltry
Webby	Hankie	Poopie
Plinky	Janky	Pissy
Plunky	Xander	Threnody
Ghoulie	Junky	Musty
Knifey	Dunkie	Megatron
Slippy	Barfy	Jandek
Frozey	Pantsy	Zoogz Rift
Flubby	Clockie	Old Man
Murky	Faxy	

14.3: COMMON AGES OF CHILDREN

Three years old	Four years old
Nine years old	Seven years old
Eight years old	One year old
Five years old	Eleven years old
Ten years old	Twelve years old
Two years old	Six years old

STEP TWO: EXPLAINING YOUR PRACTICE

Once the children are assembled before your workbench, introduce yourself and explain that you will be sharpening a pencil for them in real time. You should reassure them that there will be no trickery involved in the events that follow — that you will point the pencil honestly, without the aid of computer-generated imagery, distracting sound effects, or market-tested emotional manipulation. These savvy consumers will appreciate your pledge of hardscrabble authenticity.

Next, **show the children the pencil sharpener** you have chosen for this "very special job."

When working with children, I use a pig sharpener with a removable snout covering the entry hole — you sharpen the pencil by sticking it in the pig's nose. (The pig's digestive system has been replaced by a sharpening blade.) My experience shows that children respond well to this whimsical device, often losing themselves in an ecstasy of unguarded giggles for five to six seconds.

STEP THREE: STICKING A PENCIL UP YOUR NOSE

If you sense the children's attention lagging, **stick a pencil up your nose**. If they seem bewildered, you can explain your behavior by reference to the sharpener in hand: "Recall that this piggy pencil sharpener works by inserting the pencil into its nose; I have done the same with my own nose. I'm being silly. React appropriately."

(Children are famously undisciplined in their focus. In this photo, despite the follies unfolding before him, the male child has been distracted by the delicate shadow-play of leaves upon the windowpane.)

STEP FOUR: UPPING THE ANTE

If the children are too young to appreciate the good-will and humor you are expending on their behalf, try smiling even wider and leaning slightly forward while **pushing the pencil farther up your nose**.[2] These subtle actions should engage their attention more fully and increase the level of enthusiasm in the room.

(Sure enough, the male child's attention has been re-engaged; newly fascinated by the merriment on display, he is putty in my hands.)

Now that you have earned the children's undivided attention, remind them that you are an adult and enjoy

[2] If you feel dizzy, you've pushed too far.

14.4: DEPLOYMENT OF UNSHARPENED PENCILS IN IMAGINATIVE PLAY BY CHILDREN (MALE)

USE OF PENCIL	GAME-CONTEXT
Gun	"War"
Sword	"Sword-fighting"
Knife	"Stabbing War"
Saber	"Pirate War"
Missile	"Geopolitical War"
Spear	"Cave War"
Shiv	"Jail War"
Magic Wand	"Wizard War"
Guitar	"Rock 'n' Roll War"
Drum Stick	"Noise War"
Regular Stick	"Poke War"
Conductor's Baton	"Orchestra War"
Ceremonial Dagger	"Human-Sacrifice War"
Trumpet	"Jazz War"
Cigarette	"Grown-Up Party War"

14.5: DEPLOYMENT OF UNSHARPENED PENCILS IN IMAGINATIVE PLAY BY CHILDREN (FEMALE)

USE OF PENCIL	GAME-CONTEXT
Hairbrush	"Community Hair Salon"
Pony	"Pony Rehabilitation Center"
Magic Wand	"Sparkling Ballet Princess Eco-system"
Thermometer	"Battlefield Nurse"
Breadstick	"Italian Restaurant Waitress"
Ballpoint Pen	"Office Businesswoman"
Unicorn Horn	"Enchanted Forest"
Lipstick	"Supermodel Training Academy"
Didgeridoo	"Supermodel Ethnomusicologist"
Object of Arbitrarily Defined Value	"Socially Mediated Dyadic Tension"
Baton	"Parade"
Microphone	"Singing Contest"
Flute	"Jethro Tull Roleplay"
Wooden Ladle	"Mommy Cooking Soup"
Baby	"Baby's Too Skinny"

certain liberties they haven't earned — which is why it's appropriate for you to push a pencil up your nose, while the same behavior on their part would be irresponsible and dangerous. If there are adult chaperones in the room, shout, "Kids, you shouldn't stick pencils in your nose because you could hemorrhage blood, damage your brain, or blind yourself."

Remove the pencil from your nose, wipe it clean, and set it aside.

STEP FIVE: PLAY-TIME IS OVER

Once you have charmed the children with your nasal whimsy, proceed to sharpen the pencil according to the technique outlined in Chapter 5. You can be certain of their continued admiration and undivided attention.

Remember to smile enthusiastically and often. Address the children by name.[3]

If your little admirers break your concentration during the sharpening process with questions, remind them that sharpening a pencil, while silly and fun, is also a somber practice that demands silence from practitioner and patrons alike. Instruct them to hold their questions until the pencil is finished, at which time they will be answered in order of oldest child to youngest child.[4]

---

[3] If you have forgotten the children's names, refer to Table 14.1.

[4] As older children generally ask more sophisticated questions, their younger peers will likely find that your answers satisfy their own unanswered questions, minimizing redundancy in the exchange.

STEP SIX: "JACK AND JILL WENT UP THE HILL TO FETCH A BAG OF PENCIL SHAVINGS"

Nothing captures a child's imagination like the sight of pencil shavings being deposited in a plastic bag. Do not deny your audience the thrill of this final flourish in the sharpening process.

If they seem confused by the shavings bag, or fail to recognize its significance, you can encourage their appreciation by announcing, "I have placed the shavings of the pencil I just sharpened for you in this bag. The sharpening process is concluded and our time together has come to an end."

If the children's visit was part of a school field trip, their teacher may be reluctant to allow them back on the school bus with freshly sharpened pencils. In this case, the tiny bags of shavings will suffice as a keepsake and a sentimental comfort in the twilit years of their old age. **Tell them this.**

Thank the children for sharing in your handiwork and escort them to the door, wishing them a happy day.

(Before they leave your workshop, emphasize to the children not to make a habit of accepting bags of unusual substances from strange adults.)

ANTIQUE PENCIL SHARPENERS: A REVERIE

An effective coping mechanism for sharpening-related stress is to imagine oneself holding a 1910 Bavarian eight-bladed Luna Pencil Pointer in a field as the late-afternoon sun caresses distant hay bales (left). Although these sharpeners now cost many hundreds of dollars, the cost of possessing one in your imagination is free, as I have proven with this photograph.

If one's attention is flagging during long hours in the workshop, re-invigorate your practice by considering the impossibly complicated and intimidating Jupiter Pencil Pointer (ca. 1906), which allowed for dozens of different cutting blades (right). With such bracing daydreams can torpor can be banished, although new mental stresses may be introduced thereby—not unlike taking a cold shower on a crowded train bound for Armageddon.

CHAPTER 15:
USING A WALL-MOUNTED
HAND-CRANK PENCIL SHARPENER

FOR READERS OF A CERTAIN AGE, THE SIGHT (and sounds) of a wall-mounted hand-crank pencil sharpener is as powerfully nostalgic as the odor of tiny milk cartons, the heft of a chalkboard eraser, or the rap of an unforgiving teacher's ruler across the knuckles.

Those happy days, alas, are long gone. Once ubiquitous in American schools, the "tin man's trophy" is an increasingly rare specimen of pencil-pointing technology.[1] Nowadays the familiar silhouette of a Boston or Sanford sharpener is more likely to cast a shadow on the wall of an abandoned classroom than an active one. If you encounter one of these devices in your wanderings and decide to use it, however, the experience can be profound.

Consider what follows a re-introduction to a set of skills that were likely central to your porfolio in the distant past, but now risk fading into the ledger of the lost arts. Let us turn our contemporary sensibilities to the wall-mounted hand-crank sharpener and rediscover what pleasures remain thereby.

Urban explorers make a habit of carrying a #2 pencil on their person in case they stumble upon a wall-mounted sharpener in one of the decrepit buildings they trespass.

There is an illicit thrill to using a long-forgotten

---

[1] "Tin man's trophy" is a common nickname for the wall-mounted sharpener because it resembles the scrotum of a mechanical man.

wall-mounted pencil sharpener in an empty room, but even the most enthusiastic sharpening-adventurist should take care to think with his head, not with his pencil. Following these steps will ensure your adventure is a happy one, and that you will indeed "live to tell the tale."

STEP ONE: ESTABLISHING VISUAL CONTACT

Scan the walls for pencil sharpeners. If the abandoned building is pitched in darkness, you can simply run your hands over the walls until you feel a pencil sharpener.

STEP TWO: INSPECTING THE DEVICE

Remove the casing to examine the pencil sharpener's blades. If the sharpener has been abandoned for years, check for nests and other signs of animal habitation.

As long as the pencil sharpener has been protected from the elements, rust and rot should be insignificant. If these conditions are present, the application of steel wool, polish, and industrial lubricant may be appropriate.

15.1: COMMON LOCATIONS OF WALL-MOUNTED PENCIL SHARPENERS: A REFERENCE FOR URBAN EXPLORERS

Abandoned classrooms
Abandoned offices
Abandoned hospitals
Abandoned laboratories
Abandoned nuclear
power plants
Abandoned
grandparents'
basements
Abandoned garages
Abandoned libraries

Abandoned artists'
studios
Abandoned warehouses
Abandoned hippy houses
Abandoned baseball
games
Abandoned lunar
dioramas
Abandoned nursing
homes
Abandoned shit-holes

Abandoned shopping
malls
Abandoned boats
Abandoned vacation
homes
Abandoned orchestra
pits
Abandoned yoga studios
Grey Culbreth Junior
High, ca. 1986

STEP THREE: PREPARING THE MECHANISM

Using a toothbrush, **remove any wood shavings, graphite residue, or animal droppings**. If an animal has made diarrhea on the sharpener blades, put on rubber gloves before cleaning.

STEP FOUR: OPTIMIZING THE SIZE HOLE

Once the blades are clean and the casing is back on the sharpener, **adjust the sizing ring** so the pencil is supported while inside the sharpener.

STEP FIVE: "THE BATTLE IS JOINED"

Gently guide the pencil into the sharpener while turning the crank to engage the cylinder blades. (The process is similar to that used with tabletop hand-crank sharpeners; see Chapters 8 and 10.)

STEP SIX: CALIBRATING YOUR EMOTIONAL RADAR

As you begin sharpening the pencil, be on the lookout for the reintroduction of any sensations you had forgotten in the years since elementary school: the slight vibratory shudder of the pencil as it makes its way further into the blades; the steady, raspy exhalation of steel and cedar as the blades rotate around the pencil to shape it; the **sudden flooding memories of a childhood optimism** that saw the future as a sunny unfurling and a limitless expanse of possibility and wonder in which you would always be the center of attention.

STEP SEVEN: EVACUATING THE PREMISES

As soon as you feel yourself overwhelmed by nostalgia and despair, **hit the panic button** and leave the area immediately.

WALL-MOUNTED SHARPENER: PLACEMENT LOWER THAN USUAL

It's not uncommon to find wall-mounted pencil sharpeners in unusual locations. The reasons why are not for us to ponder; it will suffice to use these sharpeners as they were intended no matter the circumstances of their placement.

If you decide to use a pencil sharpener mounted near the floor, there are a few steps you should take to make the encounter as rewarding as possible.

STEP ONE: PREPPING THE WORK AREA

Clean the area around the sharpener of debris and dust. Even if you didn't install the sharpener, your decision to use it means its immediate environment is now your studio and your responsibility. You should endeavor to keep it as neat and orderly as you would your own workshop. As you will be working in close proximity to the floor, it is in your interest to make it minimally filthy.

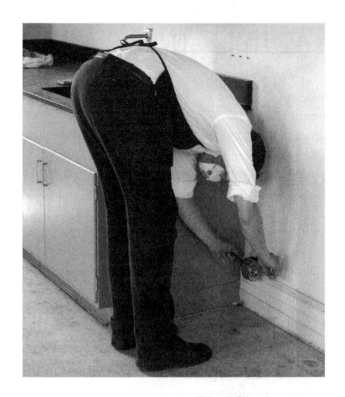

STEP TWO: GETTING IN POSITION (THREE OPTIONS)
Option One: "The Model of Efficiency"

The quickest way to use a pencil sharpener located close to the floor is to **bend at the waist** and proceed in the traditional manner. Advantages to this approach include minimal contact with the floor, minimal restriction of arm movement, and a clear line of sight relative to the sharpener. Disadvantages include significant lower back pain and the subtext of indignity.

Option Two: "The Pose of the Supplicant"

Another option is to **kneel on the floor** while supporting your weight with your elbows. This allows you to keep your back straight; it also brings your head closer to the sharpener for purposes of monitoring and inspection. Advantages to this technique include greater arm stability and increased breath control. Disadvantages include slower reaction time to threats from behind as well as a stabbing sensation in the knees and elbows.

Option Three: "Keeping a Low Profile"

This is perhaps the most straightforward approach to using a sharpener mounted within six inches of the floor. **Position yourself on the floor**, lifting your arms to engage the sharpener. Advantages of this technique include having the sharpener at eye level. Disadvantages include the necessity of an area clear of obstruction equal to the length of one's body, extended time getting into and out of position, difficulty placing the pencil in the sharpener, limited mobility, limited field of vision, minimal control over arm movement, neck strain associated with keeping the sharpener in sight, potential accumulation of floor-filth on one's smock, and excruciating pain throughout the entire body.

WALL-MOUNTED SHARPENER: PLACEMENT HIGHER THAN USUAL

Wall-mounted sharpeners are sometimes installed beyond the reach of the average user. If you encounter such a device, try accessing it by standing on your toes, as pictured here. (Standing on one's toes is an effective means of increasing one's height, if only temporarily.) If you still can't grasp the operational controls of the sharpener, it may be appropriate to make use of sturdy-ladder technology.

MNEMONIC POEM USED BY URBAN EXPLORERS TO DETERMINE WHETHER THE USE OF A LADDER IS REQUIRED TO REACH A WALL-MOUNTED SHARPENER

Can you reach it in your socks?
Can you reach it on a box?
No? Then get a ladder.

STEP ONE: GAINING ACCESS

Position a sturdy ladder underneath the sharpener, taking care to compensate for your position while using it. For example, if you plan to stand on the third step from the top of the ladder, make sure that step is a few feet to the side of the sharpener. This means you

won't have to lean too far forward or back to engage the device once you've climbed the ladder. Maintain your balance at the top of the ladder! There's no need to "be a hero" when sharpening a pencil at this height.

I cannot overemphasize the importance of using a sturdy ladder. It should be reliable, of solid construction, free of imperfections, relatively new, and incredibly sturdy, like the one pictured here.

STEP TWO: ASCENSION

Climb the sturdy ladder. Maintain eye contact with both the sharpener (lest you lose track of it and then hit your head on your target) and the ladder (lest you fall off during your ascent).

STEP THREE: "BUSINESS AS USUAL"

Sharpen the pencil as usual, keeping your center of balance over the rung you're standing on.

Do not use the pencil sharpener to support your weight. **A pencil sharpener is no substitute for a sturdy ladder!**

CHAPTER 16:
NOVELTY PENCIL-SHARPENING TECHNIQUES

EQUIPMENT CHECKLIST:

- Pencil sharpener
- Pencil (not pictured)
- Your imagination (not pictured)

THERE WAS A TIME WHEN ANY PENCIL sharpener (man or machine) was a novelty. Pencils as we recognize them have existed for centuries, yet it is only recently that pencil sharpeners have become so familiar as to lose the shock of the new.

For certain adrenaline junkies, this familiarity means a constant search for new, more radical ways of sharpening a pencil. Although one could criticize such thrill-seekers for not being content with the novelty of a well-hewn pencil that stands athwart history in our age of automation and disposability, it is perhaps more rewarding to join in the hunt.

To that end, I present here a few novelty sharpening techniques — some old, some new — that will engage both craftsman and audience.

TECHNIQUE ONE: SHARPENING A
PENCIL BEHIND YOUR BACK

This technique is said to have been inspired by Jimi Hendrix, the famous guitarist who reveled in outlandish and theatrical flourishes. One of Hendrix's signature gestures, of course, was to play his guitar behind his head.

Some argue Jimi Hendrix had to resort to playing the guitar behind his head in order to distract people from the fact that he was a mediocre musician. I disagree. Jimi Hendrix was, in fact, one of the top 500 guitar players of the 1960s. His moments of behind-the-back exuberance were actually a celebration of his talent as well as a challenge to his audience: *"If you think I'm not very good at playing guitar, how do you explain the fact that I'm currently doing so behind my head while dressed like a gypsy? No need to answer; just enjoy my interminable rock 'n' roll guitar solo."*

One of the most difficult things about playing a guitar behind one's head is that it's impossible to see the strings, frets and buttons of the instrument while doing so. The guitar teacher who begins his first lesson with "Put this

Les Paul behind your head," is not to be trusted, as the technique requires a long-established comfort and familiarity with the instrument. The same is true for sharpening a pencil behind one's back — and is why I don't recommend this novelty technique for anyone with fewer than 200 hours of sharpening experience under his or her belt.

Insert the pencil into the sharpener. **Raise your arms over and behind your head.** Don't be alarmed if you can no longer see the pencil and sharpener; this is because they are behind you. **Sharpen as usual**, making sure the shavings don't fall inside the back of your shirt.

To the casual onlooker, of course, it looks like you're simply stretching your arms or adjusting your shirt collar. But the small, steady sound of a pencil being sharpened will complicate their theory and drive them to distraction: *"Where is that sound coming from? Is somebody sharpening a pencil in here? All I see is a guy (or gal) stretching their arms or maybe adjusting their collar."*

This is the time to **turn around** and reveal your behind-the-head handiwork to the bewildered company. A moment's glance and they will understand everything.

"How can he see what he's doing? He must have 'eyes in the back of his head!'"

TECHNIQUE TWO: SHARPENING A PENCIL "WITH YOUR TEETH"

Also inspired by Jimi Hendrix, this is a more dangerous technique that calls for focus and discipline beyond that of the behind-the-head move.

When using this technique, **take the precautions necessary** to ensure that the sharpener won't accidentally slip out of your teeth and down your throat. (Indeed, it is a testament to Hendrix's own meticulous preparation and discipline that in all his years of playing guitars with his teeth, he never accidentally swallowed one.)

Place a pencil sharpener between your teeth, biting down on it to ensure its stability while pressing against it with your tongue to keep it from slipping back into your mouth.

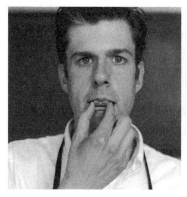 

Make sure the shavings-slit of the sharpener faces away from the mouth, so that shavings do not fall inward onto your tongue, as this could lead to panic and the accidental dislodge of the sharpener, leading in turn to choking and death. **Sharpen as usual**.

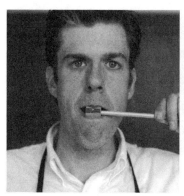 

You will notice that the gestural profile of this activity is quite similar to that of brushing one's teeth, which suggests a further escalation of whimsy: If you share a bathroom with a loved one, you can stand in front of the mirror sharpening a pencil in your mouth at the time you would otherwise be brushing your teeth. When your partner enters the bathroom, he or she will likely say, "Oh, how sweet, you're brushing your teeth, I love you" — at which time you can turn around, remove the pencil sharpener from your mouth and say, "All I can say is I'm glad you're not my dentist!" or, "Pass the Colgate — FOR MY PENCIL!"

After you share a laugh over the simple mistake, make love and ejaculate with maximum force all over the bathroom floor.

TECHNIQUE FOUR: SHARPENING A
PENCIL IN FRONT OF A CAR

This is a subtle trick, but it rarely fails to amuse. I find it hard to do without smiling.

Find a car and stand beside it, taking care not to touch it. After confirming your audience can see the car behind you, sharpen a pencil as usual.

It's difficult to say exactly why this is so appealing. Perhaps it's the juxtaposition of the staid automobile with the dynamism of pencil sharpening. More likely it's the combination of one horizontal form (the car) contrasted with a vertical form (you) holding a second horizontal form (the pencil); the mind delights in the strange mirroring effect in which horizontal forms of radically different sizes (car, pencil) are woven together by a vertical form that can smile and jump up and down (you).

Whatever the reason, this novelty technique is guaranteed to produce a pleasant sensation in the viewer—indeed, they may recall the image with a chuckle for years to come.

(A similar effect can be achieved using a bicycle, though it is less dramatic.)

Another automobile-related novelty technique, not pictured here for legal reasons, is called "The Pencil Sharpening Drive-Thru Special." In this technique, you must be *inside* a car. Order a meal at a fast-food restaurant drive-though, and then, as you pull up to the window to collect your food, **begin sharpening a pencil behind the wheel**—either using a pocket sharpener, or a handcrank sharpener you have affixed to your dashboard. "Oh hi there," you say with a grin to the astonished drive-through window employee, "I'm just sharpening a pencil at your restaurant's drive-through window." A further grace note can be added as you see fit: "Pardon me, but do you have any Grey Poupon ... for my pencil?" or "Can I get fries with that shake ... of my pencil?" (and here you shake your pencil), or "Does the humanoid accept pencil-shavings as money?" (and here you dump pencil shavings into your hand and offer them to the employee while speaking in a Martian belch-language).

TECHNIQUE FIVE: SHARPENING A PENCIL IN A WATERFALL

This is a dramatic trick, and rarely performed, as one of the necessary pieces of equipment is a functioning waterfall.

When I was hired as the on-board pencil sharpener for a Caribbean cruise, I was determined to sharpen a pencil in a Jamaican waterfall, as this is one of the "holy grails" of novelty sharpening techniques. After all, people rarely associate waterfalls with pencil sharpeners, and the juxtaposition of these two phenomena is amazing.

You will notice that I am not wearing my smock in these photographs. That is only because I had to climb the waterfall in order to reach the most picturesque spot, and didn't want to risk losing my smock in the downward plunging force of the water.

The attentive reader will also see that I am catching the shavings in my cupped hand. I never do this in my regular practice — I prefer to let shavings fall onto my workbench — but dragging a workbench into the waterfall presented issues that were beyond the scope of this project. (Needless to say, allowing the shavings to fall into the water was not an option, as the chances of successfully recovering them at the bottom of the falls were slim.)

While sharpening a pencil in a Jamaican waterfall, it is appropriate to call out to passersby: "I am literally sharpening a pencil in a Jamaican waterfall!" as I am doing here.

Here, as always, I stand behind my craftsmanship. The pencil, though damp, was sharp, and it would have taken a keen eye to notice any difference between this and any other pencil that has passed through my expert hands.

Note: Regardless of the extraordinary circumstances in which you happen to be sharpening a pencil, it is incumbent on you to do the best job you can. Whether you find yourself in a waterfall, a runaway bus, or a cave, some part of you must still be sitting at your workbench, giving your pencil the close attention it deserves. Novelty, after all, is no excuse for lackluster craftsmanship. Indeed, if people begin to associate novelty pencil-sharpening techniques with substandard results, the entire enterprise could collapse in cynicism.

TECHNIQUE SIX: THE MIND-BLOWER

This is a relatively easy trick, but don't let that blind you to the context in which it undoes one hundred years of tradition.

Its novelty is due to the fact that most pencils are sharpened horizontally, whether via pocket sharpener, hand-crank sharpener or electric sharpener. There are some contemporary electric pencil sharpeners that require the pencil be inserted vertically, but those pencils are tooled with the point facing down.

This technique's lurid appeal is that *you sharpen the pencil with the point sticking up.*

Start in the standard position for single-blade sharpening, with the sharpener secured between your thumb, index, and middle fingers. Onlookers and passersby will assume you are going to sharpen a pencil in

the traditional manner; some of them may not even stop to watch.

After capturing your audience's attention with a phrase like, "Prepare for an inversion of all that is holy," or "I'm about to straight skull-fuck your mind," **rotate your arms 90 degrees counterclockwise**, so the hand holding the sharpener is directly above the hand holding the pencil, and the end of the pencil (though obscured by the sharpener) is pointing skyward.

Sharpen the pencil by pushing gently up into the sharpener while rotating the shaft of the pencil in the traditional manner. **Let the shavings fall to the ground**.

If this technique is performed with sufficient solemnity, the awed silence of the onlookers will be such that you will be able to hear the sound of delicate cedar shavings landing on the ground like leaves in autumn. This will prime them for a lecture on the transience of life and the impermanence of all things, should you see fit.

EQUIPMENT CHECKLIST:

- Wigs
- Costumes
- Pencils
- Pencil sharpener(s)

DESPITE YOUR AUTHOR'S TIRELESS EFFORTS, live pencil sharpening does not yet enjoy the cachet of opera, professional sports, and other mainstream cultural spectacles. The aspiring professional pencil sharpener may have to be creative with his or her show in order to draw a crowd. Incorporating celebrity impressions into one's practice is a savvy way to broaden its appeal. After all, who wouldn't want to have a pencil sharpened by Al Pacino or I Love Lucy Woman?

Investing in a wardrobe of costumes and used wigs will give you the freedom to impersonate any number of celebrities. In fact, some costumes can be usefully employed for multiple impressions.

There are many occasions for **celebrity-impression pencil sharpening** (CIPS): Perhaps you have a new job and are eager to befriend your co-workers. Offering to sharpen their pencils while doing celebrity impressions allows you to break the ice and establish your reputation as a fun person. Your office-mates will laugh as you impersonate Jerry Seinfeld sharpening pencils (*"What's the deal with pencil sharpeners?"*). They'll love your impression of your new boss: *"Marcy, did you file that report about how I fart all the time? FARRRT! Whoops, I farted on a pencil."* All will be charmed, securing you a bright future at your job.

"Cher" / "Ramones"

Most people think impersonating celebrities, like sharpening pencils, is a difficult skill requiring many hours of practice and discipline. In fact, I have developed a foolproof system that allows anyone to perfect any celebrity impression in a matter of minutes.[1] If you can master the following elements, you'll have no trouble

---

[1] On the day I finally perfected this system, I got so excited I started splashing my arms and legs in the bathtub, displacing enormous amounts of water.

impersonating whoever you choose, which will introduce further levels of dynamism and excitement to your pencil sharpening.

IDENTITY SIGNIFIERS

"David Lee Roth" / "Marilyn Monroe"

It's always appropriate to begin your impression with an **Identity Signifier**. An **identity signifier** is a sentence or two that underscores your identity for your audience. When I do my impression of hip-hop music mogul Jay-Z sharpening a pencil, I begin with these words: "Hey everybody, do you like pencils and also do you like impressions?" (Pause for murmurs of excitement.) "Well, here's one … hey everybody, it's me: Jay-Z." At this point the crowd goes wild. Why? Because in announcing that I am Jay-Z, I have established my authenticity as Jay-Z, making my impression more powerful thereby. The audience now associates my Jay-Z **identity signifier** ("Hey everybody, it's me: Jay-Z") with my impression of Jay-Z, and therefore with the actual Jay-Z, as I present a totally immersive Jay-Z pencil-sharpening experience. Not only do I *tell my audience* I am Jay-Z, they *hear* that I am Jay-Z — especially in my voice when I tell them I am Jay-Z. The **identity signifier** prepares the audience for "the real Jay-Z": Me. Why? Because I am Jay-Z now.

Similarly, when I do my impression of the late public

intellectual William F. Buckley, Jr. sharpening a pencil, I'll begin: "Hey everybody, do you like pencils and also do you like impressions?" (Pause for whispers of anticipation.) "Well, here's one ... hey everybody, it's me: William F. Buckley, Jr." At this point the crowd cheers conservatively. Why? Because in announcing that I am William F. Buckley, Jr, I have established my authenticity as William F. Buckley, Jr, making

"Sir Edmund Hillary" / *"Canadian Celebrity"*

my impression more powerful. The audience now associates my William F. Buckley, Jr. **identity signifier** ("Hey everybody, it's me: William F. Buckley, Jr.") with my impression of William F. Buckley, Jr, and therefore with the actual William F. Buckley, Jr, as I present a totally immersive William F. Buckley, Jr. pencil-sharpening experience. Not only do I *tell my audience* I am William F. Buckley, Jr, they *hear* that I am William F. Buckley, Jr. — especially in my voice when I tell them I am William F. Buckley, Jr. The **identity signifier** prepares the audience for "the real William F. Buckley, Jr.": Me. Why? Because I am William F. Buckley, Jr. now.

A final example should make this clear: When I do my impression of a little baby sharpening a pencil, I'll begin: "Googoo gaga, hey everybody, do you like pencils and also do you like impressions?" (Pause.) "Well, here's one ... hey

"Olympic Medal Winner Michael Phelps" / "Nobel Prize Winner Vaclav Havel"

everybody, it's me: a little tiny baby." At this point the crowd screams. Why? Because in announcing that I am a baby, I have established my authenticity as a baby, making my impression more adorable. The audience now associates my little-baby **identity signifier** ("Hey everybody, it's me: a little tiny baby") with my impression of a little baby and with an actual, real-life baby as I present a totally immersive tiny-baby pencil-sharpening experience in my diaper.

Not only do I *tell my audience* I'm a baby, they *hear* that I'm a baby — especially in my voice when I tell them I am a little tiny baby. The **identity signifier** prepares the audience for "the real baby": Me.

Once you recognize **identity signifiers**, you'll realize that people use them all the time, as these semantic bulwarks prevent our world from collapsing into a single undifferentiated mass. Whenever you introduce yourself to someone by saying, "Pleased to meet you, I'm David Rees" (or whatever your name is), he or she perceives you as David Rees and nobody else. This makes sense because you *are* David Rees (or whoever you are) and nobody else — your use of the appropriate **identity signifier** has established that. So much so, in fact, that others will now spread the word:

Example 1:   "What's that person's name?"
"Oh, don't you know? That's David Rees."
"I guess that means he's nobody else."
"I should say so!"

Example 2:   "Class, our hero's name is David Rees. Can you think of anyone named David Rees?"
ALL: "Yes, of course: DAVID REES!"

TRIGGER PHRASES

Along with a unique **identity signifier**, any successful celebrity impression requires one or more **Trigger Phrases**: spoken cues that trigger subconscious cultural, historical, and psychological associations about a particular celebrity. They operate on a deeper level than **identity signifiers**. The right **trigger phrase** can convince an audience that they are in the presence of the celebrity associated with that phrase — it literally "triggers" their response on a subconscious level, and no rational argument will convince them otherwise.

Let's take an example from the world of politics: Bill Clinton. This former president is beloved by Americans because of his silly voice and fat nose, but he also authored many famous quotes. These quotes now serve as efficient "**Bill Clinton trigger phrases**." If I'm impersonating Bill

"Count Dracula" /
"Superman"

Clinton, I'll begin with: "Look at all these pencils I need to sharpen in the Oval Office! Oh, hello, I didn't see you there — it's me! Hey everybody, I'm Bill Clinton." (*Identity Signifier*) I will then proceed to deliver various **trigger phrases**: "I did not have sex with that woman but I feel y'all pain." (*Trigger Phrase #1*) "It depends on what's the definition of 'is.'" (*Trigger Phrase #2*) "Do the dishes, Chelsea." (*Trigger Phrase #3*) After hearing me identify myself as Bill Clinton, and then proving my bona fides with authentic quotes from Bill Clinton, the audience has been triggered to believe they are in the presence of Bill Clinton: "*I can't believe the famous president Bill Clinton is sharpening my pencil!*"

Now that the reader understands the power of **trigger phrases**, he or she should devote a few minutes to memorizing ones associated with popular celebrities. (See Table 17.1.)

"*Star Wars Robot*" / "*Star Trek Robot*"

LEARNING IMPRESSIONS PHONETICALLY

Perhaps the most effective way to master a celebrity impression is to learn it phonetically. Phonetics (the science of translating noises into English) reduces the myriad subtleties of the human voice to a standardized, easily digestible form. Memorizing the phonetic transcription of a celebrity's voice is often quicker and

17.1: TRIGGER PHRASES FOR CLASSIC IMPRESSIONS:

"I don't get no respect ... I tell ya, I get no respect ... I can't get no respect ..." (*Rodney Dangerfield*)

"Well, well ... there you go again ... jellybeans ... Russia ... government is not the solution, it's the problem of welfare queens driving Cadillacs..." (*Ronald Reagan*)

"Let's cook a chicken ... let's bake a cake ... look at this slimy cheese ... I'm cooking on TV ... good Lord, I'm like eight feet tall!..." (*Julia Child*)

"In Domingo Cristus ... everybody stop having so many abortions ... Summa Cum Laude ... some of you are having twenty abortions per week ... enough is enough ... Happy Easter from the Magic Kingdom..." (*the Pope*)

"The answer, my friend, is blowing on the wind ... play me a song, you're the Tambourine Man / play me a song toniiight ... WHEE WHURR WHAAAH (harmonica solo)..." (*Bob Dylan*)

"Welcome to Fresh Air, I'm Terri Gross ... Umm, err, that's so interesting ... I love your new book about worms ... this is NPR ..." (*Terri Gross*)

"To be or not to be, that's a good question ... 'tis better to live or die, who knows ... my dad's a ghost, ghostbusters, I'm gonna kill everyone ... I'm the king of Denmark..." (*Hamlet*)

"We love kissing and shopping ... let's drink a martini in our shoes ... hey girlfriend, did you kiss a cute guy last night?" *(The Sex & The City Girls)*

"Hallo, how are youghhh ... I am frahm Frahnce ... merci for talking to me ... have you ever been to Paris, it's one of our towns..." (*The President of France*)

"I starred in 'Pretty Woman,' the movie about the charming whore who loves to fuck and suck ... what famous American actress am

I? Yes that's right, I'm Julia Roberts ... here's my million-dollar tooth..." (*Julia Roberts)*

"Hey, everybody, how's everybody doing, it's me: Rosie." (*Rosie O'Donnell)*

"Capitalism ist evil ... yah, yah, means of production ... kill all zee rich people ... communism ist zo great ... efferybody, it's me, Karl Marx ... give me a bunch of free money..." (*Karl Marx)*

"Little Kaylene McDaniels has been missing for two weeks, where is the DA's office on this case? I think she's been murdered, don't you? The witnesses said they saw a BLUE CAR outside Kaylene's school; why don't they arrest Tony the repairman — everybody knows he drives a blue car!... I don't want to think about that little girl getting stabbed and murdered and chopped up into pieces and raped in the woods, yet I can't stop thinking about it! It's an OUTRAGE — I can't even control my own mind ... who can help me control my mind ... hey everybody, it's me, NANCY GRACE!!!" (*Nancy Grace)*

"Hallo, I'll be back, the Terminator ... look at my muscles ... my big cigars ... I can be governor ... I can pick up a barbell ... yay for me, I'm a movie star ... heil Hitler..." (*Albert Schwarzenegger)*

"I'm taking off my shoes ... now I'm taking off my socks ... now I'm putting on my slippers ... now I'm putting on my indoor socks ... now I'm taking off my outdoor sweater ... now I'm putting on my indoor sweater ... now I'm folding my outdoor sweater..." (*Mr. Rogers)*

"Harrumph ... blood, sweat, and tears ... we shall fight them on the beaches, in the air, underground, and on top of our mountains ... World War II, harrumph ... long live the Queen .." (*Winston Churchill)*

(Robot voice) "What is your search term ... feeling lucky?... here are the results ... thank you for clicking my computer button ... I can see you in your underwear." (*Google.com)*

"West Side Story Man" / "Johnny Cash" / "Computer Hacker"

"Satchel Paige" / "Joe Montana"

"Regular Mustard" / "Honey Mustard"

more rewarding than trying to mimic his or her voice by ear.

Try this simple exercise: Listen to a recording of your favorite celebrity talking. Pick those **trigger phrases** you want to master and write them out phonetically, paying close attention to the unique qualities of the celebrity's vocal patterns. The next time you're doing CIPS for an audience, instead of trying to remember how the celebrity's voice sounded on the recording, simply recite the phonetic spelling of the phrases. Your audience will be spellbound.

Some examples of phonetic transcription should make this technique easier to understand:

PHONETIC IMPRESSION: ROBERT DE NIRO

Our first specimen is required in any celebrity impersonator's portfolio: Robert De Niro in "Taxi Driver." One of that film's unforgettable moments is the infamous "mirror scene," in which De Niro's character ("Taxi-Driver Joe") yells at his reflection while admiring his new clothes.

He delivers the immortal lines:

"You talkin' to me?"

(Yoo TAL-kin' tuh MEH-uhr?)

Then he says, *"Who are you talkin' to? Hmm?"*

(Hoo-UR are yah tel-KIN' tyoo? Hrrmgh?")

"I don't see nobody else!"

(Ah DUHN'T seh no-BAWDY ulse-UHR! Hggmm.)

Finally, the scene ends with DeNiro's character saying:

"I'll see you soon in my magic mirror."

(Ah'll see YUH soon-eh in muh MAHR-jick Mir-mmm-ROWR-uhr. Hggmmrrr.)

PHONETIC IMPRESSION: SEAN CONNERY

Whether playing James Bond or one of his many lesser roles, Sean Connery always speaks with authority, thanks in part to his absurd Scottish accent. A strong Sean Connery is a must for any impressionist.

From "James Bond: You Never Live Twice":

"The name is James — James Bond."

(Th' NAME ish JAY-mesh — Jay-mesh BONED.)

"May I please have another martini?"

(Mee-YUH I pleesh HOVE a-NEUTER moir-TEY-neh?)

From "The Untouchables":

"If they pull a knife, you pull a gun!"

(IF-uh thoy puh-OOL eh knife-UH, you puh-OOL a GUN-uh! Hggmr.)

"That's Chicago for ya."

(THOUGHTS chir-CAR-goo FAHR yeh.)

From "The Hunt For Red October":

"Let's go for a ride in my submarine."

(LOTS-huh goo FAIR uh RYE-duh in moy SHOB-moy-REIGHN-uh.)

I trust the reader will find everything he or she needs to know about mastering celebrity impressions in the preceding pages, and will find pleasure and financial reward by incorporating CIPS into his or her public pencil-sharpening practice.

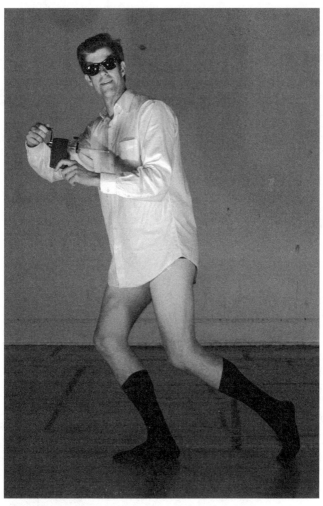

"Tom Cruise, 'Risky Business'" / "Forrest Gump" / "Runaway sex maniac" / "Honey Mustard"

CHAPTER 18

HOW TO SHARPEN A PENCIL
WITH YOUR MIND

EQUIPMENT CHECKLIST:
- Candlestick
- String
- Hair clippings
- Pencil

ALTHOUGH THIS BOOK HAS FOCUSED ON traditional pencil sharpening tools and techniques, there are additional pencil-pointing strategies available to the advanced practitioner.

Readers are encouraged to explore the use of these other technologies once they have mastered the ones covered in this text. The chisel, wood planer, CNC lathe, broken wine glass, and dog's mouth each offer unique satisfactions and outcomes when applied to a pencil.

There is another advanced technique, however, that begs for inclusion herein, only because it represents the most esoteric and demanding tradition of "putting point" to a pencil. Mastery of this technique will confirm one's status as an elite member of the pencil-sharpening fellowship.

It is the technique of sharpening a pencil with your mind.

STEP ONE: PREPARING YOUR INSTRUMENT

I trust this book has made it clear that keeping your pencil-sharpening instruments in fine working condition is crucial to the success of any given technique. In this case, the sharpening instrument is your mind, and as such must be treated to the same close attention and maintenance as that demanded by the pocketknife or the double-burr cylinder mechanism.

How well you do know your own mind? This is, no doubt, a sobering question. Yet it must be answered before proceeding. The utility of any tool is defined, in part, by consistency in deployment and predictability of outcome — the absence of unforeseen surprises once it is in use. A pencil sharpener whose blade engages erratically is no asset and should be culled from your tool kit. So, too, is a mind whose unseen contours hide jarring or potentially compromising impulses, memories, panics, prejudices, weaknesses, and the like.

Therefore we begin by applying the magnifying lenses, whetstones, and cleaning rags of our mechanical practice to our mental interiors — the better to identify, re-shape, and polish any imperfections that could keep a pencil from achieving its ideal point via this technique.

Ask yourself these questions: How often are you surprised by unbidden thoughts of a nefarious or unproductive nature? Are you able to monitor and regulate your emotional and intellectual impulses? Can you will away familiar phobias? What about unfamiliar phobias? How far into your past can you remember, and with what clarity? How far into your future can you imagine, and with what confidence?

And most important, these two questions:

1. *When you picture an object much smaller than yourself, how much detail can you pick out, and with what accuracy? What about at the microscopic level? The molecular?*

2. *How strong is your will?*

You should have definitive responses to these questions. If the workings of your mind remain as hidden and inaccessible as those of an electric pencil sharpener, there's no use in proceeding. Instead, you should **endeavor to strip away your mind's opacity**. Investing in a few years of close study and meditation will reward you with a deeper understanding of this, the most important tool in your sharpening arsenal.

You'll know when you're ready.

STEP TWO: SCHEDULING THE PROCEDURE

As this pencil-sharpening technique involves more preparation than most, you should pick your "day of appointment" well in advance.

You will need a room with natural light and plenty of circulation. The room should be absolutely dry; run a dehumidifier a few days ahead of time to be sure.

You should give up caffeine for 48 hours before the sharpening event. Heavy or fatty foods should also be avoided, as should music with heavy bass frequencies and the handling of coins. Reading, speaking, or thinking in a language other than your mother tongue could also limit the technique's efficacy.[1]

If at all possible, avoid contact with people older than you for one week prior to the event.

If you have moles, hide them with bandages before entering the room where the sharpening will take place.

Cover the room's electrical outlets before proceeding.

STEP THREE: PREPARING THE PENCIL

All sharpening techniques require that the pencil be secured against sudden or erratic movement so as to minimize irregularities in the point. This technique is no different. Although no physical blades are involved, it is imperative that your pencil remains completely still throughout the process.

Place the pencil upright in a candlestick. If the

---

[1] People raised in bilingual homes may have trouble with this technique; they are encouraged to explore other options.

candlestick is wider than the pencil, you can wrap masking tape around the eraser to ensure a snug fit.

This process, known as "**candlesticking**," is akin to setting a jewel — although our jewel has yet to assume its final form.

You should use a candlestick that has emotional significance for you. (I use a family candlestick that reminds me of my parents' unknowable youth as well as the end of an important relationship.) If you don't have access to an emotionally significant candlestick, **buy a candlestick and do something emotionally significant with it**. It doesn't matter if the emotion conjured by the experience is shame or pride, frustration or contentment, lust or dread, as long as it's highly charged and difficult to put out of your mind.

You shouldn't be able to look at the candlestick without feeling a swell of emotion.

STEP FOUR: "A GESTURE TOWARDS ST. JEROME AND ACHARYA HEMACHRANDRA"

Religious history boasts a proud tradition of asceticism and the body's physical destruction in the service of spiritual perfection. In a college course on world religions, I was struck by the story of Bodhidharma, the founder of Zen Buddhism and "Blue-Eyed Barbarian" who is said to have meditated until his arms and legs fell off. My own upbringing in the Episcopal church taught me to associate liturgy and prayer with a Jazzercise-like program of squatting, rising, kneeling and sitting on hardwood pews designed to focus the mind by numbing the lower extremities.

Although sharpening a pencil with one's mind is not religious *per se*, it does involve the exercise of metaphysi-cal techniques that have some parallel to spiritual practice. As such, it should come as no surprise that it requires at least a gesture of self-laceration; a nod to our flagellant forebears.

Use a sharp pair of scissors to cut a few locks of your hair. You don't need much.[2] It's important that a casual observer be unable to notice any difference in your appearance.

STEP FIVE: PLACING YOUR HAIR AROUND THE CANDLESTICK

Place your hair around the candlestick, a process known as "candlehairsticking."

[2] You won't need more than could fit comfortably in a shavings bag.

You have literally "locked" in your target: The pencil is now surrounded by your body's detritus, which serves

as a biological analogy to pencil shavings and a foreshadowing of your own mortality.[3]

(Every traditional pencil-sharpening technique produces physical waste as the pencil point is formed. This technique is unique in that no physical waste exists at any point — the process of candlehairsticking is needed to satisfy the law of Conservation of Mass as established by Antoine Lavoisier.)

STEP SIX: ESTABLISHING THE CONDUIT

Although this process is based on mental and supramental abilities, its success requires a physical connection between your body and that of the pencil. It's best that this connection is indirect, as direct physical contact with the pencil and/or candlestick could become noticeably painful when you least expect it, leading to shock and the project's sudden abandonment.

This point should be emphasized: ***Do not abandon this project once you have undertaken it***. *The moment you cut locks from your hair in the room is the moment you have set yourself down a path that cannot be foreshortened or diverted.*

---

[3] The foreshadowing is more pronounced if, like me, you have grey hair.

Tie a piece of string around the shaft of the pencil. The string should bind the pencil about one-third of the way down, establishing a target for your concentration.

You will notice that the string marks a line well below that of a traditional collar-bottom. That is because this process does not produce a traditional collar-bottom.

STEP SEVEN: TAKING THE STRING IN YOUR MOUTH

Place the free end of the string in your mouth so it rests comfortably on top of your tongue. Keep your mouth closed throughout the process. Breathe through your nose.

It is time to begin the sharpening process.

Your first task is to slowly un-know the candlestick in front of you. This will be difficult given its emotional significance, but you mustn't be discouraged.

Once you are completely alienated from the object holding the pencil in position, **turn your mind to the following Four Reflections**:

1. FIRST REFLECTION: Reflect upon the shepherd who stumbled upon the natural phenomenon that gave birth to the modern pencil: the massive graphite deposit in Borrowdale parish, England, discovered in the early

to mid-16th century. Cast your mind back to accompany that humble and long-forgotten man as he first ran his fingers over the extraordinary substance — still the strongest and purest graphite ever found, occurring as "large masses within mineralized pipe-like bodies, in late graphite–chlorite veins, and disseminated through the volcanic host rocks," and boast-

ing "the greatest variety of crystalline graphite morphologies recognized to date from a single deposit."[4] You are with the shepherd now, present at the wellspring of the modern pencil, the lodestar of this final practice.

2. SECOND REFLECTION: Reflect, for the first time, on a property of the hexagonal pencil not yet addressed in this book: the impossibility of a perfectly straight collar-bottom. The boundary where the straight sides of the hexagonal pencil shaft bend into the edgeless curve of the conical point is always marked by scalloping. Reflect upon the formula for calculating the area of a cone.[5]

3. THIRD REFLECTION: Reflect on the pencil

---

[4] Barrenechea, J. F., F. J. Luque, D. Millward, L. Ortega, O. Beyssac and M. Rodas. "Graphite morphologies from the Borrowdale deposit (NW England, UK): Raman and SIMS data." Contributions to Mineralogy and Petrology 158.1 (2009): 37–51.
[5] $\frac{1}{3} \pi r^2 h$

before you with increased depth, until you can navigate within the molecular structure of graphite.

4. FOURTH REFLECTION: Imagine a candle that darkens the room in which it burns.

STEP EIGHT: "WHEREOF ONE CANNOT SPEAK, THEREOF ONE MUST BE SILENT"

After a few hours of quiet reflection, it will become clear that the time for engaging the sharpening mechanism has arrived. The Four Reflections will converge, and the light refracted thereby will change within you — from a muddy warmth to a stainless, blazing beam. You will feel a burning. You may notice that the string in your mouth has begun to taste of graphite and cedar; that the room you're standing in feels smaller than your body. You will hear something that will help you understand, finally, why the electrical outlets had to be covered. You will panic. Relax.

Putting aside conscious thought, allow your mind to be flooded with patience, contentment, and boundless faith in the dawn-dappled glories of your new ability.

Wait.

Wait.

Relax.

Wait with an open heart.

Wait.

Your eyes are closed.

Open them.

AFTERWORD

The inspiration for this little book is a shipfitters manual I found at a second-hand shop many years ago. The 1940 volume was a guide for men learning the craft of steel ship assembly and repair.

That book begins with a passage from Longfellow's "The Building of the Ship," a poem written from the perspective of a vessel under construction. I've come to appreciate it as a declaration of hope as well as a celebration of craftsmanship.

This book ends with it.

BUILD ME STRAIGHT, O WORTHY MASTER
STANCH AND STRONG, A GOODLY VESSEL,
THAT SHALL LAUGH AT ALL DISASTER
AND WITH WAVE AND WHIRLWIND WRESTLE.

Some readers, having consumed this text, and finding their love and fascination for pencils inflamed to a feverish intensity thereby, may now be surprised by their desire to literally consume a pencil. The impulse is understandable.

However, as it is not recommended to eat pencils — or their shavings — we must search for proxies.

One strategy is to seek out wines that taste like pencils. The complexities and subtleties of fine wine make it the ideal vehicle for instantiating the complexities and subtleties of a #2 pencil. Many happy evenings can be spent in pursuit of the perfect "liquid pencil." Below are a few suggestions for beginning (or appending) your cellar.

A NOTE ABOUT TECHNIQUE: Pencil shavings were collected in an odorless container and presented to a wine-store owner and culinary institute graduate, who smelled them and opened bottles of wine with similar bouquets.

Château Saint Julian 2006 Bordeaux Supérieur AC
WINE EXPERT'S COMMENTS: "I'm getting a stoniness here, it's not sweet. There's a mineral core to the flavor, which is due to the vintner's hands-off approach — they're not over-cropping or reducing their grape output, which would have led to more concentrated fruitfulness and less concentrated pencilfulness."
PENCIL EXPERT'S COMMENTS: "Yeah."

Château Greysac 2007 Médoc AC
WINE EXPERT'S COMMENTS: "This wine is from Bordeaux, like the Château Saint Julian (above); it's smoother, though, with less graphite bite. I think the 'pencil smell' we're going for has more to do with the graphite and clay in the pencil point than the

cedar in the pencil shaft. That makes sense because a lot of these wines are grown in stony regions with heavy clay deposits."
PENCIL EXPERT'S COMMENTS: "Goddamn this tastes good!"

Domaine du Deffends 1992 "Clos de la Truffière" Coteaux Varois AC

WINE EXPERT'S COMMENTS: "This is a blend of syrah and cabernet sauvignon. There's a hint of graphite underneath the mushroom (which is so big and explosive on the nose), but this tastes more of cedar. I'm not surprised; as wines age, their edges are polished away and their cedar-y qualities are accentuated."
PENCIL EXPERT'S COMMENTS: "It was really nice of you to open this old bottle of wine from 1992. I appreciate it."
WINE EXPERT'S COMENTS: "No problem."

Antonio Vallana 2008 Spanna Colline Novaresi DOC

PENCIL EXPERT'S COMMENTS: "The bouquet is very graphite-y, but the actual wine tastes very grape-y and yeasty."
WINE EXPERT'S COMMENTS: "If you want to taste pencil, go with a dryer wine."

Marc Ollivier 2010 "La Pépie" Cabernet Franc Vin de Pays du Val de Loire

WINE EXPERT'S COMMENTS: "Mineral-y, red cherry with a hint of graphite — chalky and refreshing. A nice essence of pencil in this bottle."
PENCIL EXPERT'S COMMENTS: "Yeah, I smell the chalkiness which reminds me of pencil shavings. Also the label is funny — it has a drunk chicken on it. Although I cannot endorse intoxication while sharpening pencils, I recognize it may be an accidental byproduct of tasting pencil-wines and also I feel like the chicken and me are friends."

Marc Plouzeau 2009 "Rive Gauche" Chinon AC

WINE EXPERT'S COMMENTS: "Initially this wine is very sulphury. As it aerates, though, we lose the pencil shavings on the nose."

PENCIL EXPERT'S COMMENTS: "What does 'aerate' mean?"

WINE EXPERT'S COMMENTS: "See how I'm swirling my glass? I'm introducing air into the wine."

PENCIL EXPERT'S COMMENTS: "I love how much you know about wine."

Caves São João 2007 "Porta dos Cavaleiros" Dão DOC

WINE EXPERT'S COMMENTS: "Touriga nacional is another grape that frequently offers that sense of graphite and chalkiness that you get in a pencil. This is a Portuguese red, and they're a good bet for pencil flavors — especially those with the touriga nacional grape."

PENCIL EXPERT'S COMMENTS: "This tastes like pencil shavings! And it's cheap. This is my go-to wine from now on."

General advice from a wine expert regarding pencil-tasting wines: "A wine is always going to *smell* more like a pencil than *taste* like a pencil. That's just the way it is. Having said that, look for French reds from the southwest part of the country, particularly Bordeaux. Avoid white wines, because they almost never taste like pencils. As a bottle of wine ages, its edges are softened, and more interesting aromatics — secondary characteristics — emerge, and that's a good place to look for those pencil-shaving flavors. So buy older wines if you can. Ask for bottles from more traditional producers, because they tend to use larger, older barrels — which have more of the natural, cedar-y quality that is so beloved in a freshly sharpened pencil. (Bursts into laughter.)"

APPENDIX:
RECOMMENDED WEB RESOURCES

www.artisanalpencilsharpening.com
Your author's web site.

www.bleistift.memm.de
"Any old pencil won't do"
A British web site featuring reviews of pencils and writing products that may not be readily available to the American consumer. Well designed and informative.

www.branfordhouseantiques.com
"A Historic 1850s Farmhouse on a Scenic Vermont Dairy Farm"
One of the few antique stores specializing in vintage pencil sharpeners. The web site offers clear photographs from multiple angles and historical information. (The owners provided the vintage devices in this book. A trip to their store is highly recommended.)

www.fieldnotesbrand.com
"I'm not writing it down to remember it later,
I'm writing it down to remember it now."
High-quality, American-made notepads, pencils, and other writing ephemera. Co-proprietor Aaron Draplin is a great raconteur and lover of pencils.

fredspencils.wordpress.com
"I have been a glutton for pencils, that's for sure.
With this blog, I pause to burp."
Astonishing collection of vintage pencils collected over the course of 30 years. Large color photographs paired with informed commentary. When this site launched in 2011, it blew the online pencil community's mind.

matthewjamestaylor.com/blog/the-art-of-sharpening-pencils
This artist and designer's web site has a legendary page on different pencil-sharpening techniques.

www.officemuseum.com/pencil_sharpeners.htm
Wonderful catalog of antique pencil sharpeners, including photographs and production information. Many profitable hours can be spent ogling these devices.

pencilreviewer.blogspot.com
"An independent guy who loves pencils, writing about them, reviewing them, promoting the use of them, sharpening them ... He loves the smell of them, the feel of sharpening and using a vintage pencil ... You get the idea."
Exhaustive reviews of pencils and erasers.

www.pencilrevolution.com
"Pencil Philosophy: Wooden Wisdom, Product Reviews & Ephemera, etc."
One of the web's most popular pencil sites featuring interviews, vintage advertisements, and reviews.

www.penciltalk.org
"exploring the art and science of pencils since 2005"
Product reviews and industry news; home to some of the web's liveliest pencil-related discussions. Probably the best pencil web site in the English-speaking world.

www.woodclinched.com
"For the love of pencils"
General-interest pencil blog maintained by a former employee of the California Cedar Products Company (who, in turn, publish www.pencils.com).

PILGRIMAGE SITES FOR THE PENCIL ENTHUSIAST: A CHECKLIST

☐ **The Cumberland Pencil Museum**
Southey Works
Keswick, Cumbria
CA12 5NG
United Kingdom
Located only ten miles from the site of the Borrowdale graphite deposit, this is perhaps the most important pencil museum in the world.

☐ **The Paul A. Johnson Pencil Sharpener Museum**
Hocking Hills Regional Welcome Center
13178 State Route 664 South
Logan, OH 43138
Paul Johnson collected thousands of pencil sharpeners during his lifetime. He also built a custom shed to house them. After his death, the collection was moved to the Hocking Hills Welcome Center. If you are reading this book, and you live near Columbus, and you have not visited this museum, spare a moment to consider the unfortunate direction your life has taken. Then take your car keys in hand.

☐ **"Pencil City, U.S.A."**
35°29'20"N 86°27'8"W
Shelbyville, Tennessee (population: 20,335[1]) has been in the pencil business since World War I, thanks to the region's former abundance of juniper ("red cedar"). Although the glory days of American pencil production now languish in the past,

---

[1] 2010 Census data

Shelbyville can still pride itself on being home to the Musgrave Pencil Company, one of the few producers of #2s left in the United States.

☐ Grey Culbreth Junior High School
225 Culbreth Road
Chapel Hill, NC 27516

My strongest memories of using a wall-mounted sharpener date from my 7th grade pre-algebra class. I used the device constantly. My teacher delighted in my comings and goings, sparing no opportunity to remark on my preternatural sensitivity to pencil points. I thought we had established an ideal relationship until he called my mother in for a meeting in which I was reprimanded for sharpening my pencils too frequently! I remember flushing with bewilderment as he insisted the reason I constantly sharpened my pencil was because I enjoyed disrupting the class, monopolizing everyone's attention with my pilgrimages — not to mention the amusing and pleasant comments I made while traveling to and fro. I was (and remain) skeptical of my teacher's theory; I can only speak to the satisfaction I felt every time I returned to my seat with the sharpest pencil in the room — a pencil which could sometimes maintain its point for five minutes before needing to be re-tooled by the device inconveniently located in the corner of the room farthest from my desk.[2]

☐ Eberhard Faber Pencil Company Historic District
47 - 61 Greenpoint Avenue (and surrounding area)
Brooklyn, NY 11222

The former site of one of Brooklyn's most important pencil

---

[2] If this book serves any purpose, let it be as the definitive counter-argument to my teacher's conspiracy theories: Mr. Stewart, it was *always* about the pencil point.

factories, this suite of buildings in the post-industrial playland of Greenpoint is notable for its massive terra-cotta pencil reliefs. No other structure in New York boasts such handsome facades; indeed, "pencil fever" still happily afflicts many of the neighborhood's residents — some of whose relatives worked at the factory until it closed in 1956. The tumultuous family history of the Eberhard Faber company (now Faber-Castell AG), as well as its centuries-old rivalry with German rival Staedtler Mars GmbH, is more thrilling than any spy novel. For some.

☐ **Fancy Pencil Land**
801 Civic Center Dr #142
Niles, IL 60714
No artisanal pencil sharpener's life is complete until he or she can say, "I have been to Fancy Pencil Land." Fancy Pencil Land is nestled in a Korean shopping mall outside Chicago. It specializes in Asian school supplies. (I bought the pig sharpener used in Chapter 14 during a visit to Fancy Pencil Land.) Many stores specialize in Asian school supplies; only one has the greatest name of any business in human history.

APPENDIX:
HELPFUL ADVICE FROM THE
(ST. PETERSBURG) FLORIDA EYE
CENTER'S WEB SITE, REPRINTED
IN ITS ENTIRETY

If an object, such as a stick or a pencil, gets stuck in your eye, do not pull it out. Put a loose bandage on your eye. This is very serious. You need to go to the doctor right away.

THANKS TO:

Margaret and Philip Rees, for their support; **Mike Houston**, for the posters; **Meredith Heuer**, for the photos; **Chris Minney**, for the web site; **Melville House**, for the book; **Christopher King**, for the design; **John Hodgman**, for the foreword; **Kassie Evashevski**, for the contract; **John Kearney**, for the consultations and antique-sharpener photos; **Melissa Flashman**, for her encouragement; **Daniel London**, for his apprenticeship; **Aaron Gray & Liz Tomasetti**, for the records; **Emily Dougherty & Sean McDonald**, for the movies; **Sam Anderson & Sarah Uzelac**, for the food; **Tim Buzinski & Mei Ying So**, for the wine; **Jonathan Coulton**, for the cruise; **Eric Stephan**, for the waterfall photos; **Branford House Antiques**, for the vintage pencil sharpeners; **Sophie Schulte-Hillen**, for the El Casco; **Sarah Lariviere**, for her patience; **James Philip Rees**, for eating kale

Ralph Newstead, author of "Audels Shipfitter's Handy Book: A Practical Treatise on Steel Ship Building and Repairing for Loftsmen, Welders, Riveters, Anglesmiths, Flange Turners and All Ship Mechanics With Illustrations Showing Current Practice," for the inspiration

The City of Beacon, NY, for its empty high school

The United States Census Bureau, for the job.